MILITARY VEHICLES
in detail
US Half-Tracks
M2 - M3 - M5 - M9

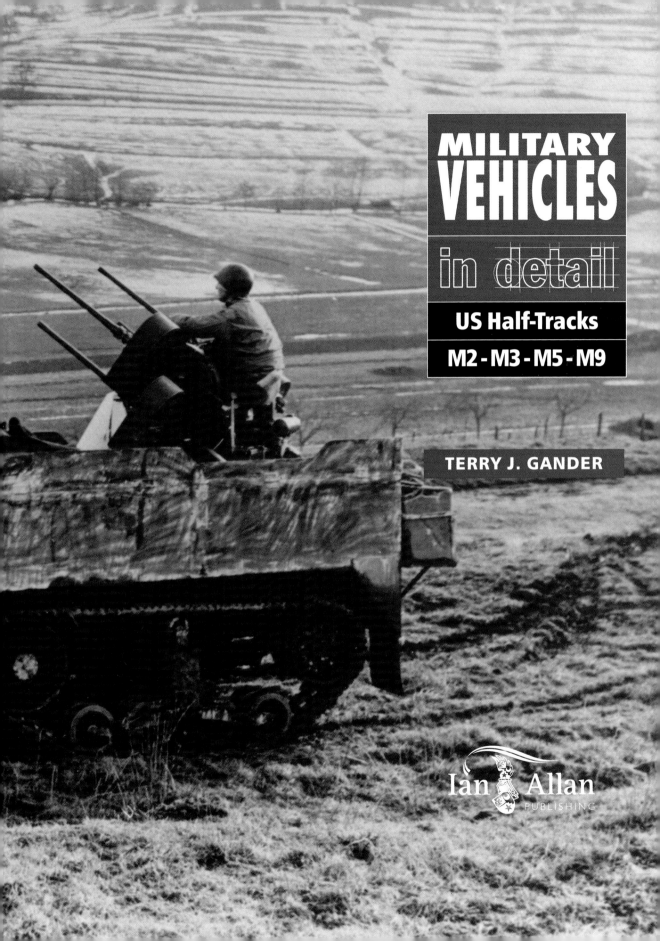

MILITARY VEHICLES in detail

US Half-Tracks
M2 - M3 - M5 - M9

TERRY J. GANDER

Ian Allan PUBLISHING

Acknowledgements

This book could not have been produced without the invaluable assistance of the following people: David Fletcher, Librarian at the Tank Museum *(TM)*, Bovington, Dorset, England, and the administrator Janice Tait, for sourcing original images and prints from archive material. Also thanks to Mike Rose for his excellent colour artworks, and John Blackman (JBn) for the use of his colour photographs.

Jasper Spencer-Smith
Bournemouth, England
May 2004

Conceived & Edited by Jasper Spencer-Smith.
Design Editor: Nigel Pell.
Illustration: Mike Rose.
Produced by JSS Publishing Limited,
Bournemouth, Dorset, England.

Title spread: Multiple Gun Motor Carriage (MGMC) M16 with 'in the field' applied winter camouflage, operating in the Bastogne area during late December 1944. *(TM)*

First published 2004

ISBN 0 7110 3047 2

All rights reserved. No part of this book may be reproduced or transmitted in any form or by any means, electronic or mechanical, including photocopying, recording or by any information storage and retrieval system, without permission from the Publisher in writing.

© Ian Allan Publishing Ltd 2004

Published by Ian Allan Publishing

an imprint of Ian Allan Publishing Ltd, Hersham, Surrey KT12 4RG.

Printed by Ian Allan Printing Ltd, Hersham, Surrey KT12 4RG.

Code: 0410/B

CONTENTS

CHAPTER ONE

Development

PAGE 6

CHAPTER TWO

Description

PAGE 22

CHAPTER THREE

Armament

PAGE 34

CHAPTER FOUR

Production

PAGE 42

CHAPTER FIVE

Weapon Carriers

PAGE 56

CHAPTER ONE

DEVELOPMENT

While the half-track concept is almost as old as the automobile itself, it found few applications, other than with a handful of specialised vehicles, until World War Two. It then became one of the most widely used of all military vehicles. It served in huge numbers with US and Allied armed forces, the US vehicles soon outstripping their German counterparts in both numbers and types.

The distinctive appearance of half-tracks came to epitomise US military activity, especially in Europe, and they continue to provide sterling service with other armies to this day, even though their origins can be tracked back to before World War One.

Kégresse

Half-tracks were under consideration almost as soon as the automobile, and especially the military automobile, was in the early stages of development. The military required cross-country vehicles that did not have to rely on hard road surfaces. By adding tracks in place of the usual rear axle(s) and wheels, some of the vehicle weight and its payload could be spread over a surface area greater than that offered by the narrow-tyred road wheels of early automobiles. It therefore became possible to provide a better degree of traction, even when traversing sand, mud and snow. Steering could be kept relatively simple by retaining the usual front wheel arrangements.

Half-tracks certainly could provide the terrain-crossing performances that their designers promoted but there was a cost. Quite apart from the mechanical complications and greater production costs, time was to show that the half-track concept combined the shortcomings of both wheels and tracks without being able to exploit fully the advantages of either. But during the early days of half-track development those adverse qualities could be overlooked, especially when no viable alternative appeared to be on offer.

Such was the case when Adolphe Kégresse, a Frenchman (some references mention his Christian name as Alexander), took up a position as the Technical Director of the Russian Tsar's various garages in the early 1900s. As with so many others, he soon came to deplore the dreadful state of the unmade paths (often mud or snow-covered) that passed as roads in Imperial Russia, and came to appreciate the low degree of automotive mobility that such rudimentary roads allowed. Kégresse therefore adopted the half-track approach although, unlike many half-track pioneers, he devised bands of rubber track in place of the metal track shoes adopted by many others. The Kégresse bands were strengthened by internal steel wire cables onto which the rubber was moulded so the resultant track was light, rugged and hard wearing while running

Above:
An example of the Citröen-Kégresse P17 as acquired by the US Army during 1931. It was a small vehicle with seating for just three passengers plus the driver. *(TG)*

Left:
The original form of the Half-Track Car T1 produced by J Cunningham, Son & Company of Rochester, New York. *(TM)*

Above:
The Half-Track Personnel Carrier T7, one of the development models that led to the M2/M3 half-track series. *(TG)*

Right:
One of the many Kégresse-pattern half-track units trialled during the early period of US development. *(TM)*

relatively quietly at high speeds. In addition the drive wheels and bogies could also be light while the track assemblies could be located on an uncomplicated spring-suspension system.

From around 1910 onwards Kégresse converted several of the Tsar's motor cars to accept his track system and he learned enough to appreciate that it offered considerable commercial potential. One of his conversions involved a Rolls-Royce that eventually became Lenin's personal transport. After 1914, Kégresse tracks were applied to some Austin armoured cars of the Russian Army, gaining more technical experience for Kégresse in the process.

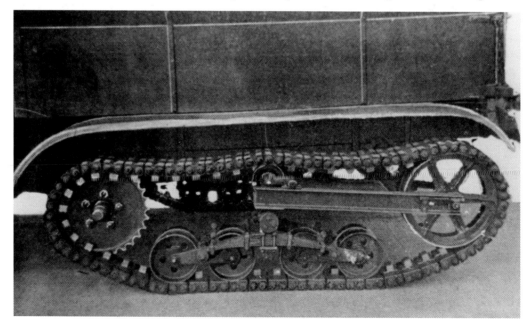

Above:
A Half-Track Car M3 undergoing field trials during 1940. Although the resemblance to the later models is apparent the body is still very basic. *(TM)*

Unfortunately for Kégresse the 1917 Revolution reduced Russia to chaos and the death of the Tsar lost him his main employer. He therefore made his way back to France via Finland. Once in France he made contact with some of his old automobile industry contacts.

One of these industrialists was André Citroën who, with one Jacques Hinstin, soon became interested in the commercial possibilities of the Kégresse track. After the financial arrangements had been agreed there followed a series of Citroën-Kégresse vehicles, some of which were to demonstrate their terrain-crossing capabilities during a series of trans-Sahara expeditions. The early Citroën-Kégresse vehicles were based on existing civilian automobile chassis, although the French military soon became avid exponents of the half-track and employed them on all manner of vehicles, including personnel and load carriers, artillery tractors and light combat vehicles.

US Developments

By the mid-1920s the US Army had also decided that the half-track was worthy of consideration. Despite the severe financial restrictions of the period the Army determined it required a light scout car for reconnaissance and general battlefield liaison duties but appreciated that even a 4 x 4 approach could not deliver the degree of terrain-crossing performance that would be necessary. Nevertheless, it continued development of the 4 x 4 approach that eventually resulted in the Scout Car M2/M3 series, whilst still seeking a viable alternative.

The search was assisted by the US Army having already gained some experience of half-tracks following the purchase of two Citroën-Kégresse tractors for towing 75mm field guns. That was during 1925 but a shortage of funds (and lack of support from an end user more interested in retaining the horse) precluded any further purchases for some years. By 1931 the US Ordnance Department had decided that the Citroën-Kégresse half-track could be a solution to its scout car mobility limitations. Rather than develop a suitable all-American vehicle from scratch just for trials, it decided to purchase a Citroën-Kégresse P17 half-track as used by the French Army. The light four-seater P17s proved so promising that a licence to manufacture the drive system in the USA was arranged. Similar Citroën-Kégresse licence production agreements were also made with Belgium, Italy and Great Britain.

Above:
A Half-Track Car M2 in early form with a skate-mounting rail for the 0.30in and 0.50in machine gun armament. The skate-mounting rail was deleted from later production examples. *(TM)*

Right:
Battle wagon for General Patton – a much modified command post version of the M2 fitted with an armoured roof and covers for the half-track units. *(TM)*

Above:
Straight from the production line, a Half-Track Personnel Carrier M2 yet to be fitted with armament and the usual storage racks. *(TG)*

Left:
Rear view of a Half-Track Car M2 showing the absence of a rear door and the stowage for the .50in M2 heavy machine gun tripod. *(TM)*

Above:
Overhead view of a Half-Track Car M5A1 with the prominent Ring Mount M49 for the .50in M2 heavy machine gun. Note the stowage for the M1903 rifles. *(TM)*

Needless to say, the home of the largest motor car industrial base in the world was not to be content with licence-building French vehicles. Instead the military adapted the Kégresse system to American vehicle designs, starting with a vehicle manufactured by J Cunningham, Son & Company of Rochester, New York. Powered by a 7,200cc V-8 petrol engine, this became the Half-Track Car T1, the first of an extensive series of experimental and developmental half-tracks of all kinds that continued throughout the early 1930s. The original T1 design was reworked at least three times which produced a series of load-carrying trucks with up to 2.5 tons (2,540kg) payloads.

Few of these development models were built in any quantity, although the track and drive systems underwent considerable refinement compared to the French original. The tracks assumed central track guides and steel cross pieces while the drive wheels became smaller and lighter. Much of the American track development work was carried out by B F Goodrich, normally associated with tyres, who also refined its track design for series production.

The Cunningham concern faded from the half-track scene after 1933. It returned to manufacturing luxury saloon cars, its place in the development chronicle being assumed by Chevrolet, Ford, the General Motors Corporation (GMC), Linn and Marmon-Herrington.

Although it was not the last vehicle in the US half-track development saga, the Half-Track Truck T9 was to make the biggest impression on the eventual outcome. The unarmoured T9 was actually a Ford V-8 1.5 tons (1,524kg) 4 x 2 cargo truck much modified by Marmon-Herrington so that drive was permanently applied to the front wheels, the drive synchronised with the tracks at the rear. The normal truck cab was retained and a standard cargo body fitted. A T9E1 duly appeared and in 1937 pilot production commenced following type classification during 1937 as the Half-Track Truck M2. Changing priorities meant that subsequent half-track truck production was limited, most

Above:
A fully-stowed Half-Track Car M3 w/winch. The canvas roof covers are in position and the windscreen covers open. *(TM)*

of the output (from Autocar) being passed to the Soviet Union under the Lend-Lease Program after 1941.

At the same time as the half-track was being developed, work was in progress on a wheeled 4 x 4 scout car that became the Scout Car M2 and M3 series, the White Scout Cars. Since half-track development had been undertaken to overcome the cross-country mobility limitations of this vehicle it made sense to combine the Kégresse-based track system used on the Half-Track Truck T9/M2 with the Scout Car M2A1.

Final development

During 1939 the White Motor Company worked with the Rock Island Arsenal to fit the half-track drive to a Scout Car M2A1 and drive train. The first result was the Half-Track Personnel Carrier T7. Successful trials conducted with the T7 led to approval for further development into the Half-Track Scout Car T14.

It was the T14 that was to form the basis of all US half-tracks that were to follow. The T14 was standardised as the Half-Track Car M2 during September 1940, and should not be confused with the Half-Track Truck M2.

The M2 was complemented in service by another half-track vehicle having a body lengthened by approximately 10in (254mm), with seating for up to 14 personnel. This personnel carrier then became the Half-Track Personnel Carrier M3 and was technically and visually similar to the Half-Track Car M2.

From these two basic vehicles all future US half-tracks were developed. At first there was a strict differentiation imposed between the M2 and M3, even though the two appeared to be similar and shared many components and sub-assemblies, including the same engine and drive train. The M2 was meant to be deployed as (among other things) an artillery tractor for artillery up to 105mm calibre and as a general utility vehicle. The larger body of the M3 was meant to act as the basis for an armoured personnel carrier, ambulance, communications vehicle and even as a weapon carrier.

Above:
Three-quarters rear view of a Half-Track Car M3 showing equipment stowage and the canvas roof covers in place. *(TM)*

Manufacture

Following the established procedures of the time (late 1940), series production of the M2 and M3 was first put out to commercial tender. In September 1940 the first production contract for M2s was issued to the Autocar Company of Ardmore, Pennsylvania, and was for 424 vehicles. The Diamond T Motor Company of Chicago was awarded a contract to produce the M3. It soon became apparent that the anticipated demands for half-tracks would rapidly become so extensive that no one company could manufacture them in sufficient numbers. The White Motor Company of Cleveland, Ohio, was therefore added to the list (it was already responsible for series production of the associated Scout Car M2A1, M3 and M3A1).

To prevent problems occurring from simultaneous production at different centres, the three main companies joined an Engineering Committee sponsored by the Ordnance Department. This committee determined the standards of design, component commonality and manufacture. Following from its deliberations, much of the basic manufacturing was to be carried out by the American Car & Foundry Company of Berwick, Pennsylvania. Further part manufacture and final assembly were carried out by Diamond T, Autocar and White, all to the same specification.

By the middle of 1941 demands from the field were already outstripping supply, especially as the Lend-Lease Act officially added many more countries to the list of potential end-users. Canada and Britain were high on this list. A new manufacturer therefore had to be added to those already established and the International Harvester Company (IHC) of Chicago, a company producing agricultural machinery, became part of the half-track production group of companies. Due to existing component supply facilities already working at full capacity, the IHC half-tracks were provided with an IHC engine, a different armoured body, and some other detail design changes, including various components and sub-assemblies not used on the original series. These IHC-related measures were tested on the M2E5/M2E6 and M3E2 development vehicles before their standardisation as the Half-Track Car M9 and Half-Track Personnel Carrier M5 respectively.

Above:
The pilot model of the multi-purpose Half-Track Car M3A2, with full stowage and equipment fitted to a standard rarely seen operationally. *(TM)*

Left:
Head-on view of the multi-purpose Half-Track Car M3A2 providing a good view of the front-mounted anti-ditching roller. *(TM)*

Above:
A Half-Track Car M3A1 closed down ready for action but with the canvas overhead covers still in place. *(TM)*

Right:
For some reason this soldier is using the bonnet of a Half-Track Car M3A1 for aiming the .50in M2 machine gun. The weapon leaning next to him is a .30in Browning Automatic Rifle (BAR), a weapon normally associated with the infantry. *(TA)*

Above:
A fully-stowed Half-Track Car M3A1 with anti-tank mines stowed in the side racks and covers for the infantry troop's M1903 rifles. *(TM)*

The IHC half-tracks were the last to enter production, all output being concentrated into 1943. Although the M9 was standardised, all IHC production was of the M9A1 with a Ring Mount M49 (see below) for a .50-calibre M2 HB machine gun.

Final Models

Once in production, half-tracks rolled off the assembly lines in thousands. The number of variants and sub-types also grew in profusion as production continued and operational requirements changed. One of the more noticeable results of combat experience was the provision of a Ring Mount M49 for a .50-calibre M2 HB heavy machine gun over the co-driver's seat, resulting in the M2A1 and M3A1 (and the corresponding IHC M9A1 and M5A1). This machine gun mounting was added to provide a more effective measure of all-round low-level air defence.

Perhaps the most significant change was initiated during early 1943. By then it was evident that there was no real need for two different types of half-track body and that all likely requirements could be met by combining the two models into one based on the larger capacity bodies of the M3/M9A1 and concentrating all further production on that model.

The development of this 'combined' version of the half-track series became the responsibility of IHC from March 1943 onwards. The result was the Half-Track Car T29, based on the M3A1 but with numerous modifications to allow it to be adapted to suit numerous end purposes. The T29 was standardised as the Half-Track Car M3A2 during October 1943. Even though the M3A2 did not enter production (by the time it appeared half-track production was already beginning to slow down) many reworked vehicles were later brought up to M3A2 standard. With the standardisation of the M3A2 all earlier M3 models were then automatically reclassified as Limited Standard.

Further modifications to the M3A2 were planned and would have been the M3A4 and M3A5. It appears that none of these latter two models was completed as by the time it would have been ready half-track production was in the final stages of winding down.

Above:
A restored Half-Track Car M9A1 w/winch still 'in action' during a recent military vehicles display. *(JBn)*

Right:
A restored example of a Multiple Gun Motor Carriage (MGMC) M16 w/winch. *(JBn)*

Above:
A restored Half-Track Car M9A1. Note the raised windscreen covers and the prominent Ring Mount M49. *(JBn)*

Left:
Back on the beaches, a Half-Track Car M3A1 configured as a command or communications vehicle. Note the prominent aerials. *(JBn)*

Above:
A heavily-laden Half-Track Car M3A1 soon after landing on the Normandy beaches, June 1944. *(TM)*

A similar programme to that for the M3A2 was carried out with the IHC Half-Track Car T31, based on the IHC M5A1 and standardised as the Half-Track Car M5A2. The interiors were so arranged that the number of troops carried could vary from five to 12, according to vehicle role. Although the M5A2 was meant to be intended for 'International Aid Requirements' (ie Lend-Lease Program), none was actually manufactured. However, the earlier M5/M5A1 and M9A1 were automatically reclassified as Limited Standard.

Almost as soon as the 'unification' programme was under way (mid-1943) it became apparent that the requirement for yet more half-tracks was diminishing. Not only had more than enough been manufactured to meet any likely future requirements but the cost and other shortcomings of the half-track concept had become much more apparent. From 1944 onwards the US Army determined that fully-tracked tractors and personnel or weapon carriers would carry out the roles previously carried out by the half-tracks.

By the end of 1943 production of the M9A1 model had ceased, while production of the other half-track models had been terminated by the end of 1944. Some facilities were retained to re-manufacture worn and battle-weary examples to the latest standards. Due in no small part to the numbers produced, and to the continuing need for such vehicles in the combat areas, the US half-tracks were still in front-line service when the war ended. The M3A1 was still listed in a US Army inventory dated March 1964 but by then there can have been few left in anything approaching active service. By 1964 the US half-tracks had been largely disposed of in one way or another. Today, half-tracks remain in the inventory of several nations, including Mexico and Israel, although in ever-declining numbers.

The final US production total for all half-track models and types was a substantial 41,169. The number of models and types was over 70, including experimental and trials vehicles. More variants were devised in the field or at local level, or to meet some national requirement. The years after 1945 added yet more variants to the overall total. (For instance, many user nations replaced the original petrol engines with diesel units.) Within these pages the main models up to the end of the war in 1945 are included.

Above:
Half-Track Car M5 w/winch with canvas roof covers in position, windscreen covers raised and anti-tank mines in the side racks. *(TM)*

Left:
A British Army Half-Track Car M5 configured as a front line ambulance – for this role no armament was carried. *(TM)*

CHAPTER TWO

DESCRIPTION

As there were over 70 variants of the basic US half-track it will not be possible to describe all types within this chapter. The description that follows is for the two main personnel carrier models and the International Harvester production equivalents.

The basic half-track layout could carry numerous types of body or weapon but apart from the IHC-manufactured models, the basic chassis, engine and drive train arrangements were standard throughout, considerably assisting manufacture and the subsequent logistic and maintenance support.

Chassis and Body

The basis of all half-track models was a modified heavy-duty truck chassis arranged so that the usual drive shaft to the rear wheels was altered into a shorter component (known as a jackshaft) that extended only as far as the forward, driving ends of the two half-track assemblies. The chassis frame was used as the foundation for a bolted-on welded steel framework onto which the main body was added.

On the M2 and M3 the body was formed by flat, face-hardened steel armour panels .25in (6.3mm) thick at the front, sides and rear. Panels of the same thickness were also provided to protect the engine and radiator, the panels being secured to the framework using bolts and self-locking nuts. The resultant body structure provided protection against rifle-calibre bullets and artillery shell splinters, although overall protection was compromised by the open-top to the rear body.

The M9A1 and M5/M5A1 models manufactured by IHC differed in that their overall armour thickness was .31in (7.94mm), while the windscreen armoured cover was .63in (15.8mm) thick. This extra protection made the IHC models somewhat heavier than their equivalents manufactured elsewhere. In addition, the armour applied to the IHC produced vehicles was homogenous rather than face-hardened and could therefore be welded and rolled into shape. This led to one recognition feature that distinguished the IHC half-tracks from all others in that the rear corners, of the body, were rounded instead of being sharply angled. Another IHC recognition feature was that the front mudguards had a flat top, those on the other models being rounded.

A two-section, shatterproof glass windscreen provided a degree of frontal protection for the occupants of the driver's cab. Extra protection was added for the windscreen

Above:
The bogie and track assembly as fitted to all models of US half-track carriers and the many variants.

Left:
One of the stages involved in replacing the half-track bogie lower road wheel rollers.

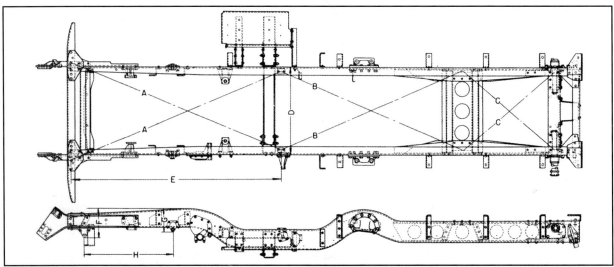

Above:
The base vehicle chassis for the half-track series, the letters relating to a dimensions table used when checking the frame for alignment. *(AN)*

Right:
Service manual close-up of the front suspension leaf spring assembly and shock absorber. *(TM)*

Far left:
The chassis and general layout was unchanged for all the US half-track carriers and variants. *(AN)*

area and two-section side-door shields by armoured steel panels .5in (12.7mm) thick. Away from combat areas the windscreen protection panel was hinged upwards and held open by support rods. Before going into action the windscreen's glass panels had to be removed before the protection panel was closed down. Vision to the front and sides was then via vision slots. Rear doors were installed only when the selected role required them - there was none on the M2. All IHC models had a rear door.

The interior of the personnel compartment at the rear differed from model to model. For the M2 there were three seats in the driver's compartment plus a further seven seats in the personnel compartment, three along each side and one in the middle facing to the rear. On the M3 there were three seats in the driver's compartment plus a further ten seats in the personnel compartment, five along each side. This seating capacity enabled each M3/M5 vehicle to carry a complete infantry section. To provide a measure of protection against the weather a canvas tilt supported by three hoops was provided with each vehicle, although it appears to have been little used while operating in combat areas.

A frame carrying a drum roller was added to the front of most vehicles to reduce the hazards of digging in when crossing ditches, banks or similar obstacles. Spring loaded to reduce contact shocks, the roller was sometimes replaced by a prominent support bracket carrying a recovery winch with a maximum direct pull of 10,000lb (4,536kg), its presence being denoted by the term 'w/winch' added to the designation. The winch was driven from a power take-off on the transfer case. Approximately a third of the final total of half-tracks manufactured were provided with this piece of equipment.

Drive

On the M2 and M3 series power was provided by a 6,320cc six-cylinder White 160AX in-line, water-cooled petrol engine delivering 147bhp at 3,000rpm (128bhp at 2,800rpm). This ungoverned engine provided a maximum recommended road speed of 45mph (72.4km/h) although higher speeds were possible. For routine purposes the maximum

(cont page 32)

Left:
Installing the track chains. These were fitted when the vehicle was required to be driven over snow, ice or muddy terrain. *(TM)*

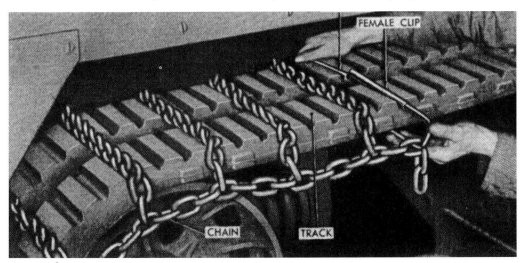

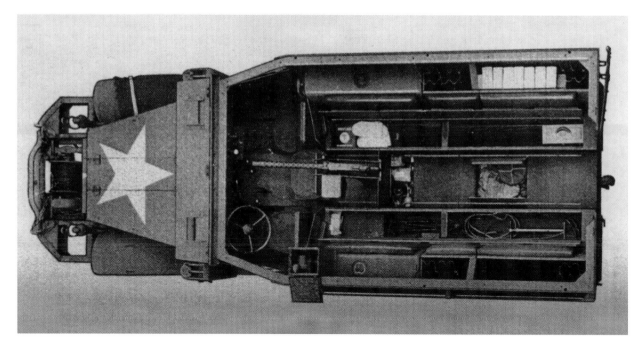

Above:
Service manual illustration of the interior and under-floor stowage compartments on a Half-Track Car M3 w/winch Personnel Carrier. *(AN)*

Right:
The equipment and accessory stowage arrangements on this restored Half-Track Car M9A1 are probably more indicative of service use rather than service manual requirements. *(JBn)*

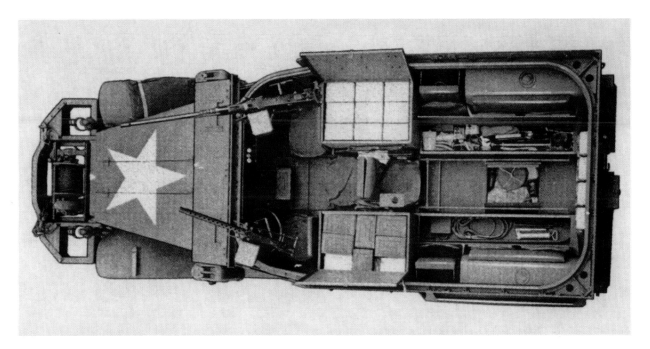

Above:
The interior and under-floor stowage compartments on a Half-Track Car M2 w/winch Mortar Carrier. *(AN)*

Left:
The winch assembly fitted to about one third of all Half-Track models. The winch had a direct-pull capacity of 10,000lb (4,536kg). *(JBn)*

Above:
Left-hand side of the IHC RED 450B six-cylinder in-line petrol (gasoline) engine installed on all International Harvester M5, M5A1 and M9A1 half-track carriers. *(GM)*

Right:
Right-hand side of the IHC RED 450B engine. *(GM)*

Left:
Left-hand side of the White 160AX six-cylinder in-line petrol (gasoline) engine which powered all M2 and M3 half-track carriers and variants. *(AN)*

Left:
Right-hand side of the White 160AX showing the exhaust manifold and the location of the carburettor positioned on the top of the engine. *(AN)*

Right:
The transmission unit and driver controls as fitted to every US half-track. The steering column can be seen above the control levers. *(TM)*

Right:
The gearshift diagram located in front of the driver to show selection position and operation of transfer case and front-wheel-drive. *(TM)*

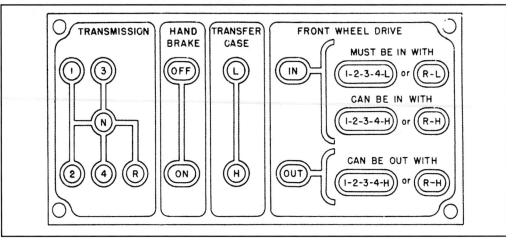

Above:
The interior of a Half-Track Car M5A1 showing the basic seating for the infantry. Machine gun ammunition would normally be stowed in the magazine box on the gun mounting. *(JBn)*

Left:
The driver's position was the same on all US half-track models and variants. The front compartment had seating for two occupants alongside the driver. *(JBn)*

speed was usually limited to 40mph (64.3km/h). Fuel consumption was from 3 to 3.6 miles per US gallon (approximately .66 to .8km per litre). Two 30 US-gallon (113-litre) fuel tanks, one each side of the crew compartment, enabled a road cruising range of approximately 175 miles (281km). The petrol (gasoline) recommended was 80 octane.

On the IHC-built M5, M5A1 and M9A1 half-track models the engine installed was a 3,790cc six-cylinder IHC RED 450B in-line, water-cooled, low-compression petrol engine delivering 143bhp at its maximum governed speed of 2,700rpm. This engine enabled a maximum road speed of 38mph (61km/h), while the cruising range was reduced to approximately 125 miles (201km). The radiator coolant capacity was also slightly increased on IHC models.

Both types of engine were coupled to a Spicer 3641 gearbox providing four forward speeds plus one reverse, with a single dry plate clutch and a two-speed transfer case. The front final-drive axle was a Timken F35HX1 split type, while that for the rear was a Timken 5641BX67 of the banjo type. Models manufactured by IHC had that company's banjo-type axles.

The two spring vertical volute suspension half-track assemblies used four pairs of small rubber-tyred bogie wheels (or rollers) with a steel double track support roller at the top. The final drive sprocket had 18 teeth. Idler sprocket wheels at the rear could be adjusted to vary the tension of the 12.75in (323.9mm) wide rubber tracks. Each vehicle was delivered with a set of track chains to be fitted to the tracks when negotiating snow or muddy terrain.

The front wheels, originally of a commercial truck type but later of military ventilated disc pattern, carried 8.25 x 20 12-ply tyres (IHC models had 9.00 x 20 12-ply tyres). The wheels were combined with a front suspension combining semi-elliptic springs with double-acting hydraulic shock absorbers. A Ross Gear TA26 cam and twin-lever steering system was provided, the minimum turning radius (driving to the left) was approximately 30ft (9.14m).

The brake system, provided by Bendix/Wagner, was hydraulic with power assistance, while for parking a hand lever was connected to a disc brake behind the transfer case. A Warner electrical trailer brake was provided for when

towing loads. The maximum cross-country towed load was 2.01 tons (2,041kg), sufficient to tow an artillery piece such as the 105mm Howitzer M2 or M2A1 or the British 17-pounder anti-tank gun.

In the cab compartment the driver was seated on the left. Driving controls were completely conventional and differed little from commercial truck practice of the period. They included a steering wheel, gearbox and front axle drive shift levers and conventional brake, clutch and accelerator pedals. Vehicles fitted with a recovery winch had a power take-off control operated by the driver. The outline shape of the instrument panel on IHC models differed from all others.

Above:
An unusual role for the Half-Track Car M2 was as a psywar vehicle used to broadcast news and other propaganda to the enemy lines. The 'announcer' on the left is reading from a script and is using a face microphone. Note the loudspeaker on the top of the vehicle. *(TM)*

Ancillaries and Stowage

On early production half-tracks the headlights were fitted on top of the front mudguards. This rendered them prone to knocks and damage so they were later relocated to between the mudguard and engine cover. The vehicle's electrical system was 12V, with a single 168Ah battery located below the right-hand door. Delco-Remy supplied the generator.

Interiors had steel or aluminium 'chequered-pattern' floor plates to reduce slipping hazards when wet. Some of these plates were hinged to provide access to storage lockers. Ammunition storage racks were provided externally on the body rear, while side racks (one each side) were provided to carry M1 anti-tank mines, 14 on the M2 and 24 on the M3. Two further side racks, one each side, were used to carry fuel or water jerricans, while combat tools were stowed below each side door.

Radio installations varied greatly according to the users involved but two were normally fitted. One was for vehicle-to-vehicle communications with another providing the command link. Command vehicles carried extra sets.

Every vehicle was equipped to carry a hand-operated fire extinguisher, plus a Decontaminating Apparatus M2 in case of chemical agent attack.

CHAPTER THREE

ARMAMENT

Nearly all US half-tracks carried some form of armament for local or air defence. In the case of infantry units, armament was employed as central fire support for both disembarked and on-board troops.

When US half-tracks were deployed as armoured personnel carriers they also acted as fire-support platforms for the disembarked troops. The main weapons fitted were machine guns but the weapon-mounting arrangements varied according to the vehicle model and battlefield deployment.

Machine Guns

When US half-track production commenced the fire-support weapon normally carried was the .30-calibre M1919A4 (flexible) air-cooled machine gun, type classified in 1919. It was a flexible mounting development of the water-cooled .30-calibre M1917, and was intended for many roles ranging from aircraft to co-axial machine gun, both weapons having been designed by John Moses Browning, one of the most prolific small arms designers of all time. The M1919A4 was a belt-fed machine gun with a cyclic fire rate of 400 to 500 rounds-per-minute (rpm). The gun alone weighed 31lb (14kg).

However, the M1919A4 machine gun was almost always supplemented by an extra, heavier machine gun, the .50-calibre M2 HB (HB - Heavy Barrel), another air-cooled machine gun designed by Browning. Destined to become one of the finest and most widely produced machine gun designs (it is still in production in 2004), the M2 was designed during the aftermath of World War One and entered mass production only during the late 1930s. The belt fed M2 was, and still is, a devastating anti-personnel and low-level air defence weapon, its main drawback being the weight of approximately 84lb (38.1kg), just for the gun alone. The cyclic rate of fire was from 400 to 500rpm.

While both these weapons could be fired from mountings on the carrier vehicle, both were provided with appropriate tripods for dismounted ground use when required. A Tripod Mount M3 was carried for the .50-calibre M2 HB, the Tripod Mount M2 for the .30-calibre M1919A4.

The M2 half-track originally carried a .30 and a .50-calibre machine gun on separate M35 cradle/carriage assemblies on a skate mounting rail that surrounded the interior of the vehicle, guns being moved around the rail as necessary. The M3 and M5 originally lacked any provision for a .50-calibre M2 HB machine gun, the only weapon provided being a single .30-calibre M1919A4 on an M25 pedestal mount secured to the floor of the

(cont page 40)

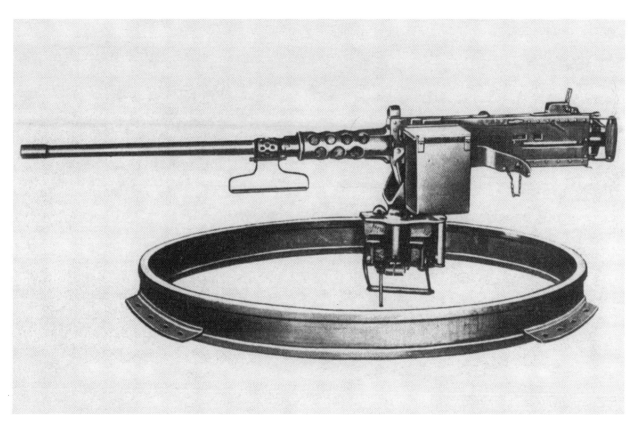

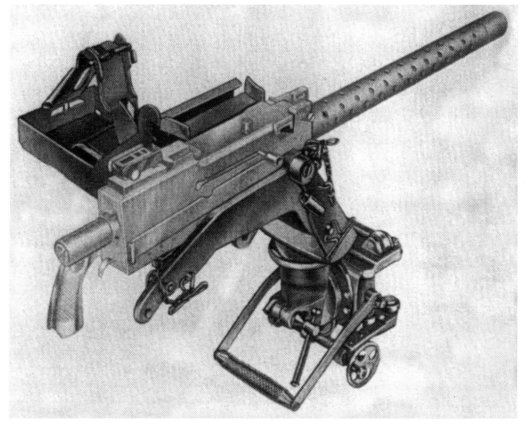

Above:
The Ring Mount M49 for a .50in M2 machine gun as installed in 'A1' series half-tracks. The belt-magazine box can be seen as well as the spade grips normally for use on flexible mountings. *(AN)*

Left:
One of the many types of vehicle mounting likely to be employed with the .30in M1919A4 air-cooled machine gun was the Machine Gun Mount M35C. *(AN)*

Above:
A fully armed Half-Track M3A1 Personnel Carrier showing the extra armour provided for the .50in M2 machine gun and Ring Mount M49. *(TG)*

Right:
A well-laden 75mm Gun Motor Carriage (GMC) M3 with the addition of a .50in M2 heavy machine gun, a weapon not normally carried on these vehicles. *(TA)*

Above:
A Free French Half-Track Car M3, during a training excercise, engaging a target with the .30in M1919A4 machine gun. *(TA)*

Left:
US Marines on Peleliu Island, October 1944, using a 75mm Gun Motor Carriage (GMC) M3 as cover during an advance. The secondary .30in and .50in machine gun armament was not normally carried on these vehicles but, as shown, has been added to provided extra fire support. *(TA)*

Left:
A Half-Track Car M2 operated by a reconnaissance unit in Tunisia. Note the .50in M2 heavy machine gun and pintle mounting. The rifle is a .30in M1903. *(TA)*

Above:
A rather unusual addition to the armament of this Half-Track Car M3 is a water-cooled .30in M1919 machine gun. The vehicle is from a US Army combat engineer unit, Italy 1944. *(TM)*

personnel compartment, but this arrangement was soon changed.

This weapon mounting changed with the introduction of the M2A1 and M3A1 models, the same changes applying to the IHC M9A1 and M5A1. The .50-calibre M2 HB machine gun was relocated to a Ring Mount M49 over the co-driver's position. This ring mounting 'pulpit' provided the weapon with a better mounting facility for low-level air defence, the weapon being capable of a full 360° traverse with barrel elevation from -15° to +85°. In addition three further fixed pintle sockets were provided for the .30-calibre M1919A4, one on each side with the third at the rear of the body.

These changes were carried over to the Half-Track Personnel Carrier M3A2. An armoured shield for the ring-mount machine gunner was produced for this planned model.

As a general rule there was stowage on the vehicle for boxes containing 7,750 rounds of .30-calibre rifle ammunition and 700 rounds of .50-calibre machine gun ammunition. The M3 model had provision for only 4,000 rounds of .30-calibre ammunition. Following the introduction of the 'multi-role' M3A2, and if a specific mission required it, a further 6,000 rounds of .30-calibre ammunition could be carried, together with a further 600 rounds of .50-calibre ammunition. If this additional load was necessary, two occupants of the M3A2 personnel compartment were not carried to provide the extra stowage space required.

The above outline concerns only the 'official' machine gun and ammunition allotments for half-track personnel carriers. Needless to say there were many other measures adopted to boost the firepower of units in the field.

Ancillaries

As the M3 and M5A1 half-track series were primarily personnel carriers, much of their potential firepower was from the weapons of the troops carried in the vehicle. (The M2 and M9 series did not normally carry infantry.) When half-tracks were first introduced, and for some time after 1941, the main US Army infantry

Above:
A column of Half-Track Car M3A1 carriers advancing through Normandy during August 1944 with the .50in M2 heavy machine gun at the ready. *(TA)*

weapon was the bolt-action Rifle, Caliber .30 M1903 or M1903A1, known almost universally as the Springfield. By 1943 the Springfields were gradually being supplemented (and eventually replaced) by two new self-loading weapons, the Rifle, Caliber .30 M1 (the Garand) and the smaller and lighter Carbine, Caliber .30 M1, M1A1 or M2. Carbines - meant to be carried by officers and NCOs but also often by other ranks - fired a different, lower-powered cartridge compared to the other rifle calibre weapons.

Each half-track driver was provided with his own personal weapon in the form of a 0.45-calibre sub-machine gun. During the early war years this was a Thompson M1928 or M1928A1, or the more easily produced M1 or M1A1. By the end of the war these .45-calibre sub-machine guns were still around in large numbers although they were meant to be replaced by the unloved Sub-machine Gun, Caliber .45, M3 or M3A1, known almost universally as the 'Grease Gun' from its crude appearance. Provision was made for the stowage of 540 rounds of .45-calibre ammunition on each vehicle.

By 1945 another weapon had been added to each M3A2's weapon load, namely a single Rocket Launcher, Anti-tank, 2.36-inch M1A1 (or the later two-section barrel M9). This light, shoulder-fired launcher, the Bazooka, could defeat the armour of the heaviest Axis tanks and was usually operated by a team of two from a ground-firing position. While powerful, thanks to the shaped-charge warhead carried by the rocket, the Bazooka was essentially a short-range weapon.

Side racks (one each side) were provided to carry M1 anti-tank mines, 14 on the M2/M9A1 and 24 on the M3/M5. These side racks were not always fitted.

Provision was made for each half-track to carry hand grenades. These were a mix of the Grenade, Hand (Fragmentation) Mk II, Smoke WP M15, and Smoke, Colored, M6 or M18, the latter being intended for signalling or position marking. The M2/M9A1 models carried 10 grenades and the M3/M5 models carried a total of 22. The proposed M3A2 and M9A2 would have carried 24 grenades.

CHAPTER FOUR

PRODUCTION

The massive numbers of half-tracks produced for the
US Army and the Allies came from the production lines
of International Harvester, White, Autocar and Diamond T.

Once the US half-track assembly lines had been established they were able to produce vehicles by the thousand. More half-tracks were manufactured than any other US armoured combat vehicle, with the sole exception of the Medium Tank M4 series.

Numbers

The total number of US half-track carriers produced between 1941 and 1944 was 39,328. A further 1,841 were manufactured to meet some special-purpose role, such as a Gun Motor Carriage (GMC), as outlined in the Variants section. Where possible, the production totals for these 'special' models are provided there.

Production by model for carriers was as follows :

Year	1941	1942	1943	1944	Total
M2, M2A1	3,565	4,735	4,102	656	13,058
M9A1	0	0	3,433	0	3,433
M3, M3A1	1,859	4,959	7,610	825	15,253
M5, M5A1	0	152	6,332	1,100	7,584
Totals	5,424	9,846	21,477	2,581	39,328

From this table it follows that the group of companies – Autocar, Diamond T and White built a total of 28,311 half-tracks. This can be compared to the output from International Harvester, namely 11,017.

As far as can be determined from official US Government figures, the total number of vehicles by model was as follows:

M2	11,415	M2A1	1,643
M3	12,499	M3A1	2,862
M5	4,625	M5A1	2,959
M9A1	3,433		

Lend-Lease Program allocations are shown below. It has not been possible to discover the allocations for the M9A1 but all production of this model was directed towards 'International Aid Requirements' or the Lend-Lease Program.

Model	British	C/wealth	Free French	Soviet Union	American Republics
M2, M2A1	10	0	31	402	11
M3, M3A1	2	40	1,431	2	3
M5, M5A1	5,238	20	0	420	12

These figures brought the known Lend-Lease Program half-track production total to 7,622. If the entire output of the M9A1 production is added the final total was 11,055.

Above:
Half-Track Car M5 as produced by International Harvester but with the armament yet to be installed. Note the protection brackets for the headlamps and the flat-outline mudguards. *(AN)*

Left:
Half-Track Car M9A1 showing the Ring Mount M49 for the .50in M2 machine gun. The mounting for the .30in M1919A4 machine gun is shown but the machine gun is not installed. *(AN)*

Above:
A British Army Half-Track Car M3 extensively modified with a hard-top box-shaped body to act as a mobile command and communication centre. *(NM)*

Right:
A Canadian Army Half-Track Car M5 with a raised roof cover fitted out as a mobile command vehicle – note the prominent aerial. *(TA)*

Standard Production Models

Model	M2	M2A1	M3	M3A1
Occupants	10	10	13	13
Gross weight	8.84 tons (8,981kg)	8.75 tons (8,890kg)	8.93 tons (9,072kg)	9.15 tons (9,299kg)
Length with roller	19.56ft (5.96m)	19.56ft (5.96m)	20.29ft (5.95m)	20.29ft (5.96m)
Length with winch	20.14ft (6.14m)	20.14ft (6.14m)	20.8ft (6.34m)	20.8ft (6.34m)
Width w/o mine racks	6.44ft (1.96m)	6.44ft (1.96m)	6.44ft (1.96m)	6.44ft (1.96m)
Width with mine racks	7.29ft (2.22m)	7.29ft (2.22m)	7.29ft (2.22m)	7.29ft (2.22m)
Height, overall	7.42ft (2.26m)	8.88ft (2.69m)	7.42ft (2.26m)	8.88ft (2.69m)
Ground clearance	11.19in (284mm)	11.19in (284mm)	11.19in (284mm)	11.19in (284mm)
Wheelbase	11.29ft (3.44m)	11.29ft (3.44m)	11.29ft (3.44m)	11.29ft (3.44m)
Ground contact length	3.9ft (1.19m)	3.9ft (1.19m)	3.9ft (1.19m)	3.9ft (1.19m)
Max road speed	45mph (72.4km/h)	45mph (72.4km/h)	45mph (72.4km/h)	45mph (72.4km/h)
Gradient	60%	60%	60%	60%
Vertical obstacle	1ft (.31m)	1ft (.31m)	1ft (.31m)	1ft (.31m)
Fording	2.67ft (.81m)	2.67ft (.81m)	2.67ft (.81m)	2.67ft .(81m)
Turning radius, left	30ft (9.14m)	30ft (9.14m)	30ft (9.14m)	30ft (9.14m)
Fuel capacity	24.86 gallons (113litre)	24.86 gallons (113litre)	24.86 gallons (113litre)	24.86 gallons (113litre)
Approx cruising range	175 miles (281km)	175 miles (281km)	175 miles (281km)	175 miles (281km)
Engine	6,320cc six-cylinder White 160AX, in-line, water-cooled petrol delivering 147bhp at 3,000rpm			
Transmission	Spicer 3641 gearbox providing four forward speeds and one reverse			
Electrical system	12V	12V	12V	12V

Left:
A British 8th Army Half-Track Car M9A1 towing a 17-pounder anti-tank gun towards the Gothic Line in Italy, 1944 . *(TG)*

Above: US Army troops training with a Half-Track Car M2 w/winch – there is no ammunition box fitted to the .50in M2 machine gun. *(TM)*

Right: Passing through a border town in Germany, 1944, the troops in this Half-Track Car M3 have added a water-cooled .30in M1919 machine gun to augment the vehicle's armament. *(TA)*

IHC Production Models

Model	M5	M5A1	M9A1
Occupants	13	13	10
Gross weight	9.15 tons (9,988kg)	9.6 tons (9,752kg)	9.46 tons (9,616kg)
Length with roller	20.18ft (6.15m)	20.18ft (6.15m)	20.12ft (6.15m)
Length with winch	20.75ft (6.32m)	20.75ft (6.32m)	20.72ft (6.32m)
Width w/o mine racks	6.44ft (1.96m)	6.44ft (1.96m)	6.44ft (1.96m)
Width with mine racks	7.29ft (2.22m)	7.29ft (2.22m)	7.29ft (2.22m)
Height, overall	7.58ft (2.31m)	9.42ft (2.87m)	7.58ft (2.26m)
Ground clearance	11.9in (284mm)	11.9in (284mm)	11.9in (284mm)
Wheelbase	11.29ft (3.44m)	11.29ft (3.44m)	11.20ft (3.44m)
Ground contact length	3.9ft 1.19m	3.9ft 1.19m	3.9ft 1.19m
Max road speed	38mph (61km/h)	38mph (61km/h)	38mph (61km/h)
Gradient	60%	60%	60%
Vertical obstacle	1ft (.31m)	1ft (.31m)	1ft (.31m)
Fording	2.67ft (.81m)	2.67ft (.81m)	2.67ft (.81m)
Turning radius	30ft (9.14m)	30ft (9.14m)	30ft (9.14m)
Fuel capacity	24.86 gallons (113litre)	24.86 gallons (113litre)	24.86 gallons (113litre)
Approx cruising range	125 miles (201km)	125 miles (201km)	125 miles (201km)
Engine	3,790cc six-cylinder, IHC RED 450B in-line, water-cooled, low compression petrol delivering 143bhp at 2,700rpm.		
Transmission	Spicer 3641 gearbox providing four forward speeds and one reverse		
Electrical system	12V	12V	12V

Left:
The helmets worn by the occupants of this Half-Track Car M2 towing a 57mm M1 anti-tank gun indicate that this combination belongs to a Free French formation, actually the Second Moroccan Division operating in Italy, 1944. *(TM)*

Half-Track Car M2A1
Scale 1:35

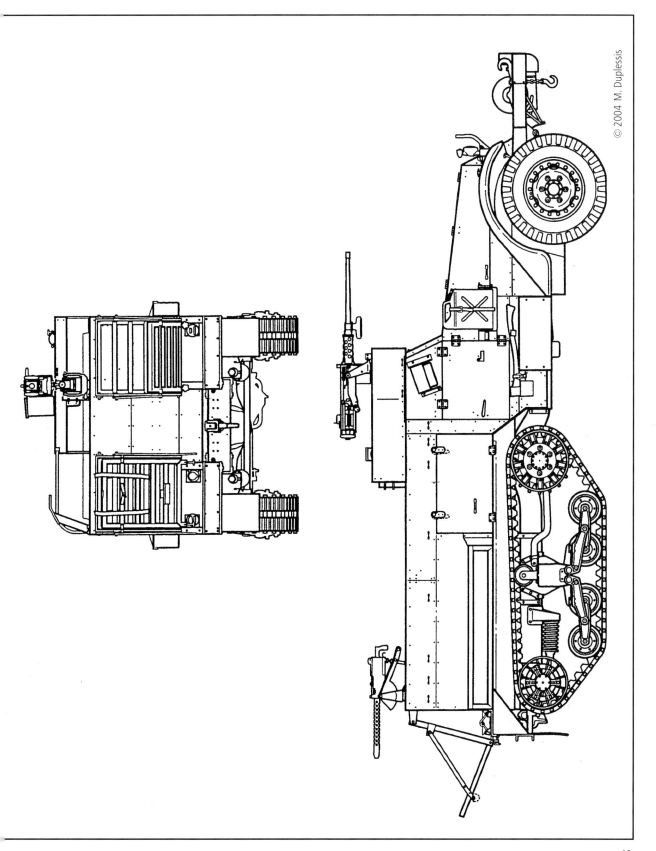

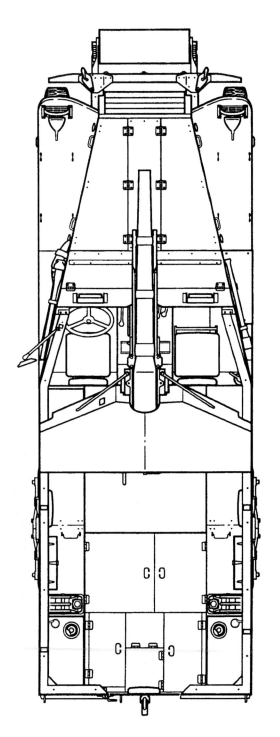
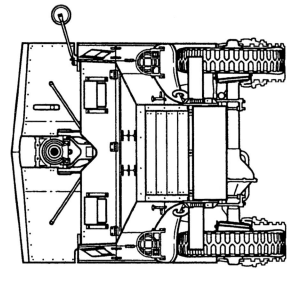

Half-Track 75mm Gun Motor Carriage M3
Scale 1:35

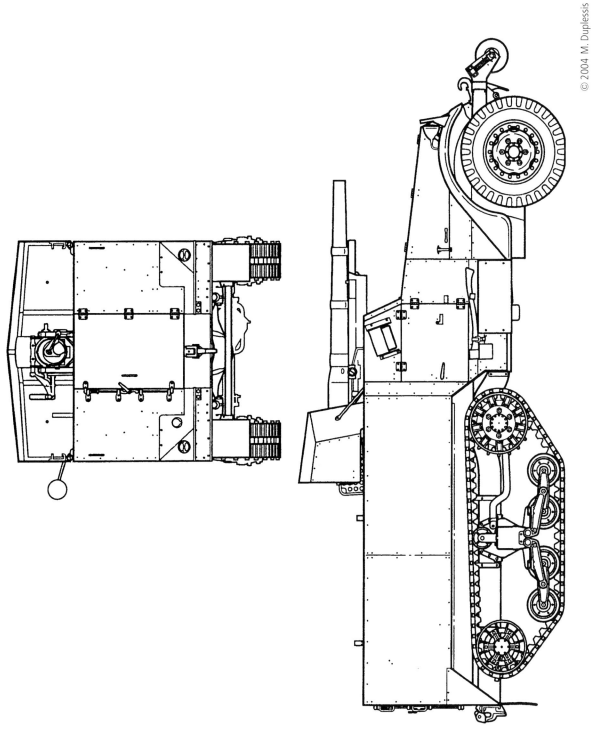

Half-Track Multiple Gun Motor Carriage M16
Scale 1:35

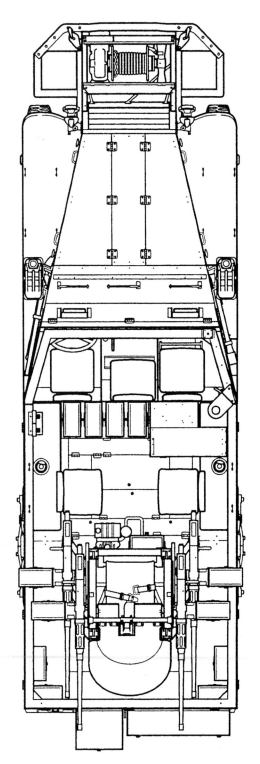
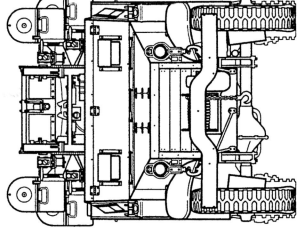

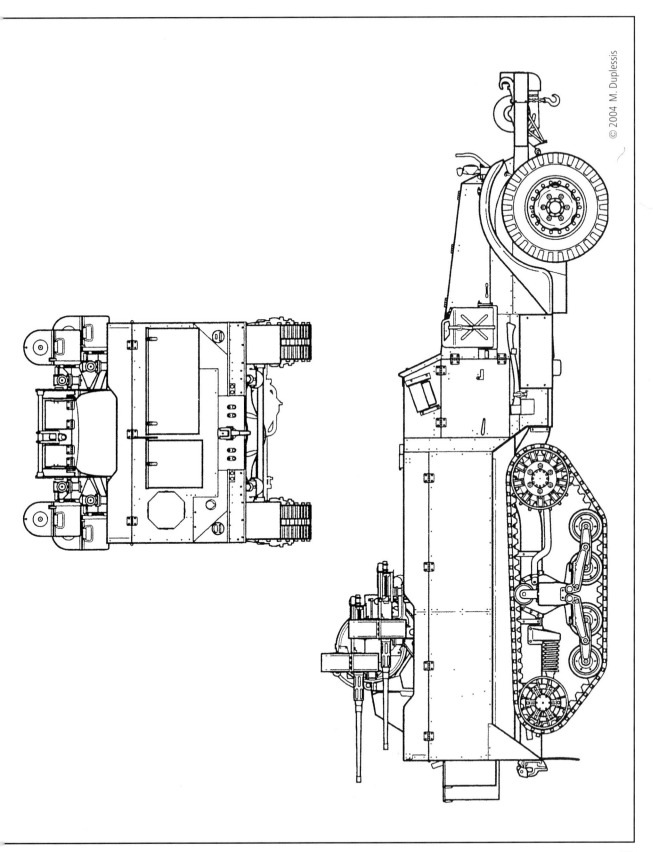

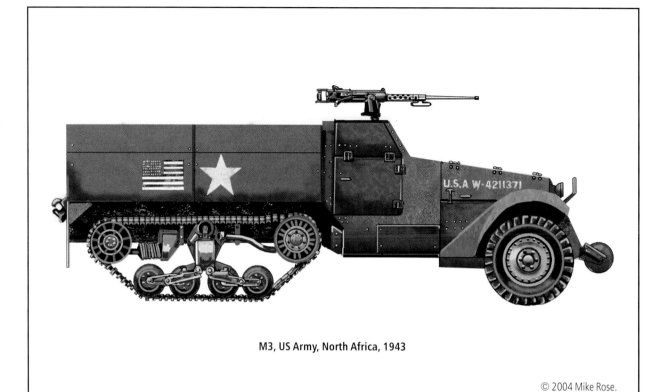

M3, US Army, North Africa, 1943

© 2004 Mike Rose.

Right:
A British Army Half-Track Car M9 fitters vehicle of C Squadron, 5 Royal Tank Regiment, towing a trailer carrying servicing equipment, Hamburg, 1945. *(TM)*

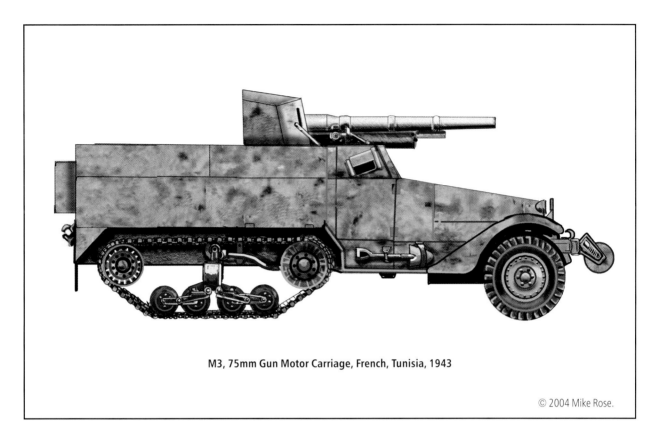

M3, 75mm Gun Motor Carriage, French, Tunisia, 1943

© 2004 Mike Rose.

British National identification

Up to 1942 (Western Desert).

1942-45.

Allied air recognition signs.

Allied air recognition.

Allied air recognition, variant.

United States National identification

Brazilian Expeditionary Force, Italy

Air recognition.

National identification mark on vehicles.

© 2004 Nigel Pell

CHAPTER FIVE

WEAPON CARRIERS

Although the bulk of the US half-tracks were built as personnel carriers with just machine gun armament they were also produced in numerous weapon carrier forms, from mortars to air-defence weapons and artillery platforms.

While some of the weapon carriers were manufactured in quantity, most were regarded as interim carriers until more suitable weapon platforms could be found.

Types

The main types of the US half-track were the carriers (already covered in a previous section). There were also Howitzer Mortar Carriers, Gun Motor Carriages, Multiple Gun Motor Carriages, Mortar Carriers and Half-Track Trucks. Of these the Mortar Carriers were the most closely allied to the basic half-track carrier vehicle.

Mortar Carriers

On the half-track Mortar Carriers the main change was that the personnel compartment was modified so that a mortar could be carried, along with a load of mortar bombs and the mortar crew. The need for some form of half-track mortar carrier to provide fire support for dismounted infantry actions had been appreciated at the same time as the other half-track carriers were in their final stages of development. The first of the type (the M4) was standardised in October 1940.

The mortar fitted to US half-track mortar carriers that actually entered production was the 81mm Mortar M1. This fired a 'light' high-explosive bomb weighing 7.28lb (3.3kg) to a maximum of 3,290yd (3,008m). Maximum muzzle velocity was 700ft/sec (213m/sec). There was also a heavier high-explosive bomb with a reduced range, also smoke and illuminating bombs. The weight of the complete mortar, with the mounting, was 136lb (61.69kg). The normal rate of fire was 18rpm, or 30 to 35rpm for short bursts.

Half-Track 81mm Mortar Carrier M4

The 1940 mortar carrier was originally seen as nothing more than a means to transport an 81mm mortar, its crew and a viable load of mortar bombs.

(cont page 61)

Above:
The Half-Track M21 81mm Mortar Carrier with winch, identifiable by the position of the mortar barrel to fire forward over a frontal arc. *(TM)*

Left:
Overhead view of a Half-Track M21 81mm Mortar Carrier showing the ammunition stowage racks and the locations of the 81mm Mortar M1 and the .50in M2 machine gun. *(TM)*

Above:
The Half-Track M4 81mm Mortar Carrier with the mortar positioned for firing to the rear. Note the skate-rail mounting for the .30in M1919A4 carried for local and air defence. *(TM)*

Right:
On the Half-Track T21 4.2in Mortar Carrier the rifled mortar was fired to the rear – on the T21E1 it was fired to the front. Later it was decided that the mortar was more suitable for heavier vehicle platforms. *(TM)*

Above:
The first purpose-built mortar carrier intended for firing from within the vehicle – the Half-Track M4 81mm Mortar Carrier. *(TM)*

Left:
The Half-Track M4A1 81mm Mortar Carrier was based on the Half-Track Car M2 but with the rear modified to allow the mortar to be fired. *(TM)*

Right:
The 81mm Mortar M1 in ground-firing configuration with a portable baseplate. This mortar was the type carried by the M4, M4A1 and M21 Mortar Carriers. *(AN)*

Below:
A Half-Track M4A1 81mm Mortar Carrier in action, Italy 1943. Note the absence of a .30in M1919A4 machine gun from the skate-mount. *(TM)*

Left:
A fully-equipped Half-Track M4A1 81mm Mortar Carrier showing the position of mortar bomb racks containing the bombs in transport containers. *(TM)*

It was intended that the mortar and crew would dismount from the vehicle for firing the mortar from a ground position using its usual bipod and baseplate. The mortar could be fired from the rear compartment but only in an emergency as the carrier vehicle was a virtually unaltered Half-Track Car M2 with no special strengthening to absorb firing stresses. Although not recommended, it was possible to fire the mortar over the rear of the vehicle and many crews did so as a matter of course, even though the barrel traverse was limited to the 14° afforded by the bipod mounting. For local defence the carrier was provided with a .50-calibre M2 HB heavy machine gun and 750 rounds of ammunition. There was no mounting on the vehicle for the machine gun - that also had to be dismounted for firing from an M2 ground tripod.

The 81mm Mortar Carrier M4 was manufactured by the White Motor Company and 572 were produced during 1942. The crew was six, and provision was made to carry 112 mortar bombs. The gross weight of the vehicle was 8.99 tons (8,098kg).

Half-Track 81mm Mortar Carrier M4A1

By early 1942 the tactical limitations of the Mortar Carrier M4, including the time it took to get the mortar into action, had become apparent so an improved model was requested. As a result, and still using the Half-Track Car M2, the

61

Above:
The Half-Track T21E1 4.2in Mortar Carrier had the 4.2in rifled-mortar firing to the front but the vehicle/mortar combination was not sucessful and the project lapsed. *(TM)*

personnel compartment floor was reinforced so the mortar could then be fired to the rear from within the vehicle. At the same time barrel traverse was increased to approximately 34°. As before, the mortar could be dismounted for ground firing. The crew remained at six. The bomb stowage capacity was decreased to 96 rounds, some of them stowed externally in ammunition boxes at the rear. A .30-calibre M1919A4 machine gun was mounted on a skate rail that enabled the gun to be moved around the vehicle. Later in the war an anti-tank Rocket Launcher AT, 2.36in, M1 (Bazooka) and ten M6 rockets were added to the weapon load. It was also possible to carry up to 14 anti-tank mines.

The M4A1 was standardised in December 1942 and reclassified as Limited Standard in July 1943. Production of the 600 vehicles was carried out by White and all were delivered during 1943. Gross vehicle weight was 7.97 tons (9,135.5kg).

Half-Track 81mm Mortar Carrier M21

Originally known as the Half-Track 81mm Mortar Carrier T19 and standardised in July 1943, this model was built around the M3 personnel carrier. Apart from the vehicle platform, the main departure from earlier practice was that the mortar was positioned to fire forwards from the vehicle over a traverse arc of 60°. The crew remained at six. Ammunition stowage was 97 mortar bombs and a .50-calibre M2 HB machine gun on a pedestal mount was standard. As with the M4A1, an anti-tank Rocket Launcher AT, 2.36in, M1 and ten M6 rockets could be carried, along with 12 anti-tank mines.

Production was again by the White Motor Company. Production ceased after 110 vehicles had been completed during 1944. A total of 54 were supplied on Lend-Lease terms to the Free French Army; they were the only such recipients. Gross vehicle weight was approximately 8.93 tons (9,072kg).

Half-Track 4.2in Mortar Carrier T21 and T21E1

The 4.2in Mortar M2 was originally developed as a special mortar for delivering smoke screening or chemical agent bombs, but once the war commenced it was found to be

Above:
A 75mm Howitzer Motor Carriage (HMC) T30 with the muzzle of the 75mm Field Howitzer M1A1 on Mount T10 at maximum depression of -9°. *(TG)*

highly effective for delivering high-explosive ordnance. During late 1942 it was decided that a mobile mounting based on the M3 personnel carrier might be of combat value, the result being the Mortar Carrier T21. The T21 was similar to the M4A1 with the mortar firing to the rear. It was then decided to follow 81mm Mortar Carrier M21 practice with the mortar firing over a frontal arc. The result then became the Mortar Carrier T21E1. At the same time the mortar base securing point was reinforced.

After testing it was decided not to proceed with the project as the 4.2in mortar was deemed more suitable for fully-tracked carriers. The T21E1 had a crew of five and weighed approximately 9.83 tons (9,072kg). A .50-calibre M2 HB machine gun on a Ring Mount M49 was provided.

The 4.2in mortar had a rifled barrel and weighed 333lb (151kg) complete. It fired a 25.5lb (11.58kg) chemical bomb to a range of 4,397yd (4,020m). The maximum muzzle velocity when firing a high-explosive bomb weighing 24.5lb (11.11kg) was 841ft/sec (256m/sec).

Howitzer Motor Carriages

The M3 half-track personnel carriers were intended to be utilised as carriers for several types of artillery calibre weapon but, as far as howitzers were concerned, they served as weapon platforms only until more suitable fully-tracked carriers became available. Two types of Howitzer Motor Carriage (HMC) were based on the M3 personnel carrier half-track, both of them developed using experience gained during the development and deployment of the 75mm Gun Motor Carriage M3 (qv).

75mm Howitzer Motor Carriage T30

The 75mm Howitzer Motor Carriage T30 was introduced to provide armoured formations with artillery fire support. The half-track was selected for the role primarily because it was available, development of a howitzer installation commencing in October 1941 at the request of the US Armored Force Board. Two pilot vehicles were built by Autocar and one underwent trials at Aberdeen Proving Ground, Maryland, commencing in January 1942.

The platform was the Half-Track Personnel Carrier M3 and the artillery piece was the 75mm

Above:
Although regarded as a short-term expedient, the 105mm Howitzer Motor Carriage (HMC) T19 was built in significant numbers (324) but it was top heavy and lacked on-board ammunition stowage. This is the pilot vehicle. *(TG)*

Field Howitzer M1A1 on Mount T10. The installation of the howitzer was straightforward and uncomplicated but various shapes and sizes of shield were tested until one .38in (9.5mm) thick was selected.

The 75mm Field Howitzer M1A1 was originally a towed gun intended for issue to horse artillery batteries. It had a short (15.9-calibre) barrel and could fire a 14.6lb (6.62kg) high-explosive projectile at a maximum muzzle velocity of 1,270ft/sec (387m/sec) to a range of 9,760yd (8,925m). The howitzer could also fire a shaped-charge high-explosive anti-tank (HEAT) projectile weighing 13.1lb (5.94kg). With a trained crew the howitzer could fire up to six rounds a minute for short periods. The more usual rate of fire was three rounds a minute. When installed on the T30, barrel traverse was 22.5° either side, with barrel elevation from -9° to +50°.

Other weapons carried on the T30 included a .50-calibre M2 HB machine gun on a modified M25 pedestal mount and four .30-calibre rifles or carbines. The driver was provided with a .45-calibre sub-machine gun. There was stowage for 60 rounds of 75mm ammunition. The crew was five.

A batch of five hundred T30s was ordered from White but the type was never standardised and retained the T30 designation throughout its service career (probably because it was regarded as an interim vehicle). All had been delivered by the end of 1942. Once in service the T30 was found wanting in terms of protection for the howitzer and crew and the cramped space in which the crew had to operate. When the 75mm Howitzer Motor Carriage M8, based on the chassis of the Light Tank M5, became available, the T30s were withdrawn, their howitzers being salvaged for other purposes. Out of the total of 500 T30s manufactured by White, 188 were converted back to M3 personnel carriers.

The combat weight of the T30 was approximately 8.71 tons (8,845kg).

105mm Howitzer Motor Carriage T19

The 105mm Howitzer Motor Carriage T19 emerged for much the same reason as the 75mm T30. When some form of mobile 105mm

howitzer platform was requested during September 1941 it was refused, but by October 1941 approval was more forthcoming. A 105mm Howitzer M2A1 was removed from its usual towed carriage, slightly modified, and placed on a modified, forward-firing 105mm Howitzer Mount T2. Although little appears to have been expected of the half-track/105mm howitzer combination, initial firing trials at Aberdeen Proving Ground gave better results than had been expected, even though the vehicle frame became slightly distorted during firing. It was therefore recommended that production examples should be suitably reinforced. A batch of 324 T19s was ordered to be manufactured by Diamond T, and all had been delivered by the end of 1942.

The 105mm Howitzer M2A1 had a 22.5-calibre barrel and fired a 33lb (14.98kg) high-explosive projectile. When fired from the T19 at a maximum muzzle velocity of 1,550ft/sec (472m/sec) the maximum range was 11,700yd (10,699m) when using the highest possible angle of barrel elevation. When installed on the Mount T2 the barrel elevation arc was from -5° to +35°, while the barrel traverse was 20° each side.

Other weapons carried on the T19 included a .50-calibre M2 HB machine gun on a modified

Below:
An early example of a US Army Howitzer Motor Carriage (HMC) T19. Note the crew wearing 1941-pattern steel helmets. The open nature of the howitzer installation is clearly shown. *(TG)*

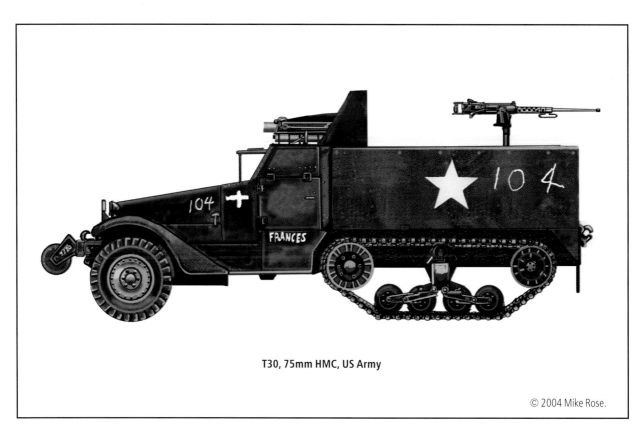

T30, 75mm HMC, US Army

© 2004 Mike Rose.

M3A1, North-West Europe, 1944, US Army

© 2004 Mike Rose.

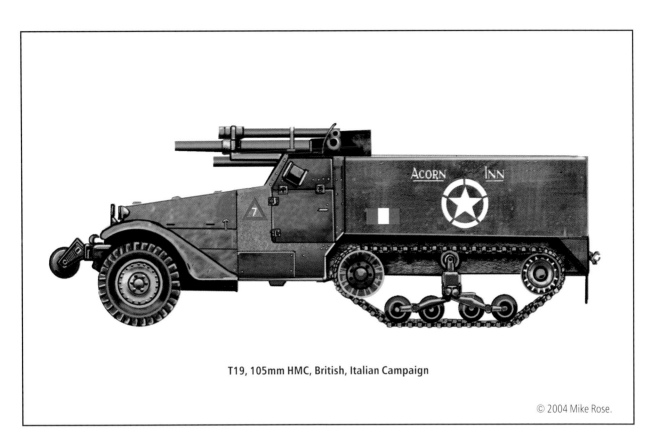

T19, 105mm HMC, British, Italian Campaign

© 2004 Mike Rose.

M3, 75mm GMC, British, Italian Campaign

© 2004 Mike Rose.

Above:
Two British Army 75mm Gun Motor Carriage (GMC) M3s in action somewhere in Italy during March 1945. *(TM)*

M25 pedestal mount and four .30-calibre rifles or carbines. The driver was provided with a .45-calibre sub-machine gun. There was stowage for just eight rounds of 105mm ammunition. The crew was six, five of them crewing the howitzer.

As with the 75mm T30, the 105mm T19 was never standardised, even though it did see service during the US Army's operations in North Africa and Sicily. However, most never left the US, being retained for training purposes. By 1943 the T19 had been withdrawn and replaced in armoured formations by the 75mm Howitzer Motor Carriage M8. The T19 had always been regarded as a short-term expedient and proved to be not entirely satisfactory for providing fire support for armoured formations. Once in service it proved to be somewhat top heavy and unstable, while the working area for the gun crew was restricted and largely unprotected. Perhaps the most serious shortcoming was that the quantity of ready-use ammunition carried was too limited for most fire missions, leading to the need for ammunition carriers to be always in attendance. But the T19 was, for its time, better than nothing.

There were also the 105mm Howitzer Motor Carriage T19E1 and T19E2. The T19E1 was provided with an armoured shield over the mounting while the T19E2 carried a 105mm Howitzer T7, much the same gun as used on the T19 but with a shorter barrel. Neither the T19E1 nor the T19E2 progressed further than single prototypes of each type.

The combat weight of the 105mm T19 was approximately 9.83 tons (9,072kg).

Gun Motor Carriages - Anti-tank

The term Gun Motor Carriage (GMC) was applied to two main categories of weapon, mainly anti-tank guns and air defence guns.

US Army anti-tank gun motor carriages were originally designed as tank destroyers. During the 1930s the tank destroyer was very much a US concept as for various reasons, mainly because of the country's isolation from armoured warfare developments elsewhere, the US Army came to believe that in any future wars tanks would not fight tanks. Tanks were expected to act either as cavalry scouts or to support infantry operations. Staff officers

Above:
A US Marines 75mm Gun Motor Carriage (GMC) M3 coming ashore from an LCT (Landing Craft, Tanks) during the Pacific campaign. *(US Army)*

devised the theory that any enemy tanks that might appear would be neutralised either by anti-tank guns or lightly armoured and highly mobile self-propelled gun platforms. The latter became known as tank destroyers, their doctrine and organisation being promulgated by an Army directorate known as Tank Destroyer Command, with its own specific equipment procurement procedures.

The problem for Tank Destroyer Command was that as late as 1941 it still had no tank destroyers to command. When it became apparent that war was approaching, emergency measures to provide some form of tank destroyer were introduced. There were two main results, one being the placing of a 37mm anti-tank gun on a Dodge 4 x 4 truck chassis. This became the Gun Motor Carriage M6 saw action in North Africa but its shortcomings meant that thereafter it was primarily used for training or as a disarmed utility vehicle. The other, more successful, result was the mounting of a 75mm field gun on a Half-Track Personnel Carrier M3. The latter eventually became the 75mm Gun Motor Carriage M3.

75mm Gun Motor Carriage M3 and M3A1

The starting point for the 75mm Gun Motor Carriage M3 was the developmental 75mm Gun Motor Carriage T12. It was a straightforward fitting of a 75mm M1897A4 gun on a pedestal mounting secured at the front of the usual personnel compartment of an M3 carrier. Work on this conversion began in June 1941, leading to standardisation as the Gun Motor Carriage M3 in September 1941.

The 75mm M1897A4 gun concerned was originally a towed field gun of French design. It had been adopted by the US Army soon after it became involved in World War One during 1917. The M1897A4 was a US reworked variant that appeared during the 1920s and 1930s but by 1941 most had been withdrawn from service. By 1941 there were considerable numbers of these guns available from reserve stocks so yet another artillery/half-track expedient was created. The 75mm gun could fire an armour-piercing capped (APC) projectile at a muzzle velocity of 2,000ft/sec (609m/sec) with enough power to penetrate 3in

Above:
A battery of camouflaged British Army 75mm Gun Motor Carriage (GMC) M3s in action firing against Ravenna, Italy, during early December, 1944. *(TM)*

Right:
A US Marine 75mm Gun Motor Carriage (GMC) M3 coming ashore on Trokina Cape, Bougainville Island, in the Solomons, 1 November 1943, during the Pacific Campaign. The 75mm GMC was particularly effective against Japanese defences. *(US Army)*

(76mm) of face-hardened steel armour at 1,000yd (914m). In 1941 this performance was better than most available anti-tank weapons could achieve so the gun was considered as suitable for the tank destroyer role.

The T12 was standardised as the 75mm Gun Motor Carriage M3 during November 1941 and went into production (by Autocar) almost immediately. The M3 differed from the T12 mainly in the type of gun mount located behind an armoured gun shield .5in (12.7mm) thick. This gun mount was initially an adaptation of the 75mm Gun Carriage M2A3 known as the Gun Mount M3. When supplies of the M2A3 carriage ran out they were substituted by the 75mm Gun Carriage M2A2 which was then adapted to become the Gun Mount M5. Vehicles with the M5 mount became the 75mm Gun Motor Carriage M3A1.

On the M3 vehicle with the Gun Mount M3 the barrel elevation limits were from -10° to +29°, with traverse being 19° left and 21° right. On the M3A1 vehicle with the Gun Mount M5 the barrel elevation limits were from -6.5° to +29°, with traverse being 21° either side. When firing forwards at low elevation angles the windscreen had to be folded down onto the engine covers. Another difference between the two gun mounts was that on the M3 the traversing and elevating handwheels were both on the left-hand side of the gun. On the M5 the aimer could operate the traversing handwheel only as the elevation handwheel was on the right-hand side of the gun.

The production total for the M3 and M3A1 finally reached 2,202. Of these, 86 had already been completed by the end of 1941, just in time for some of them to be sent to the Philippines before the islands fell. The figure for 1942 was 1,350 plus a further 766 during 1943. Production then ceased, due mainly to the stocks of surplus guns being exhausted. The M3/M3A1 was finally declared as obsolete in September 1944. By then the M3/M3A1 had been issued to the US Marine Corps to take part in the various operations of the Pacific War. British Army batteries operating in Italy were also provided with the M3/M3A1, although these equipments do not appear among available Lend-Lease records.

The Marines deployed the M3/M3A1 in the role that it soon acquired, that of direct fire support during armoured and infantry operations. The myth that tanks would not fight tanks was soon exploded and the 75mm gun rapidly became ineffective for its intended tank-killing task. The 75mm M3 and M3A1 were therefore diverted away from the tank destroyer role towards that of an artillery fire support weapon. The M3/M3A1 performed sterling service in this role as the 75mm gun could fire a high-explosive projectile weighing 14.6lb (6.628kg) to a range of 13,595yd (12,431m) as well as also firing armour-piercing ammunition. The ammunition stowage capacity was 59 rounds.

The M3 and M3A1 did not carry any secondary armament other than the five-man crew's personal rifles or carbines.

There was also a prototype 75mm Gun Motor Carriage T73. It was similar to the M3 but the gun involved was the 75mm Gun M3, as issued for the Medium Tank M4 series. It did not progress very far before being abandoned as unnecessary.

The combat weight of a Gun Motor Carriage M3/M3A1 was approximately 8.93 tons (9,072kg).

Above:
The 57mm Gun Motor Carriage T48 carrying a 57mm Anti-Tank Gun M1, the US Army version of the British 6-pounder. *(TM)*

57mm Gun Motor Carriage T48

Development of the 57mm Gun Motor Carriage T48 was initiated during April 1942, the intention being to produce a useful carrier for the 57mm Anti-Tank Gun M1. It was originally expected that the T48 would be manufactured to fill both US and British Army requirements but in the event the bulk of the completed vehicles were allotted to Britain, and most were then diverted to the Soviet Union.

The main reason for the general all-round non-acceptance of the T48 was the gun involved. The 57mm Anti-Tank Gun M1 was a rare example of the US Army adopting a British weapon. By late 1940 it was apparent that something heavier than the US 37mm Anti-Tank Gun M3A1 (then the only dedicated US anti-armour weapon) was going to be needed to defeat the ever-improving armoured protection being applied to Axis tanks. Adopting the British 6-pounder anti-tank gun was an easily-accommodated emergency solution and it went into US production during early 1942, at almost the same time as the British original.

The gun performance certainly looked impressive. It could fire a 6.28lb (2.83kg) projectile at a muzzle velocity of 2,800ft/sec (853m/sec) and penetrate 2.2in (55.6mm) of face-hardened armour at 1,000yd (914m). It seemed to be a logical measure to combine the gun with a mobile platform so, using the experience gained with the 75mm Gun Motor Carriage M3, the M3 personnel carrier was modified accordingly.

Under the direction of the Ordnance Department at the Aberdeen Proving Ground, a 57mm M1 gun was placed on a Mount T5 behind the protection of a face-hardened steel gun shield 0.63in (15.88mm) thick at the front and .25in (6.35mm) at the sides and top. Barrel elevation was from -5° to +15°, with traverse being 27.5° either side. Stowage was provided for 99 rounds of 57mm ammunition and the vehicle carried a crew of five.

By the time the T48 had entered production in October 1942 (manufactured by White) matters had changed. The US Army had by then decided it no longer had any requirement for

Above:
A US Army Multiple Gun Motor Carriage (MGMC) M16 at the liberation of Rennes in France, August 1944. *(TM)*

the T48 so all output was for the British to the extent that detail design changes to suit their particular requirements were introduced. These changes included, among others, racks for five British Lee-Enfield rifles (the only secondary armament on the T48) and provisions for a British Wireless Set No.19. It then transpired that the British no longer had any interest in the T48 either, as the gun's armour penetration performance had already been outmoded by the introduction of even heavier armour on German tanks.

But production still continued into 1943, the final total being 962. Of these 680 were allotted to Britain on Lend-Lease Program terms but once again priorities changed and the British accepted only thirty T48s. Even those few eventually had the guns removed for conversions to other, non-gun, roles. With US agreement, the remainder, totalling 650, were diverted to the Soviet Union where the T48 was known as the SU-57. An example still exists at the Kubinka Museum in the outskirts of Moscow.

Of the 312 retained on a Limited Procurement basis in the US, an undetermined number, but probably all, were converted back to M3A1 personnel carrier standard.

The combat weight of the 57mm Gun Motor Carriage T48 was approximately 8.84 tons (8,981kg).

Gun Motor Carriages - Air Defence

As far as half-track air defence Gun Motor Carriages, as opposed to Multiple Gun Motor Carriages, were concerned there was only one type of gun involved, the 40mm Automatic Gun M1 - the Bofors Gun. Exactly how the US armed forces came to adopt the 40mm M1 in preference to their home-grown 37mm Automatic Gun M1A2, of which more later, is a lengthy saga. Suffice it to say the better-performing Bofors Gun came to be preferred over the 37mm M1A. Due to prior commitments to the 37mm gun and a chronic shortage of virtually all types of military equipment, the 37mm gun was maintained in

Above:
The 40mm Gun Motor Carriage T54, the chassis of which proved to be too overloaded and unstable for firing the 40mm Gun M1. *(TG)*

production until sufficient 40mm guns became available. As matters turned out both types of gun were still in service when the war ended.

As early as 1940 it was decided to develop self-propelled carriages for both the 37mm and 40mm air-defence guns. The resultant development histories were somewhat chaotic as all manner of fully-tracked and half-tracked platforms were used for trials. It has to be said that none of the half-tracked 40mm Gun Motor Carriages proved satisfactory and none passed the prototype stage. The first prototype appeared during June 1942.

The 40mm Automatic Gun M1 was used for all the associated mobile half-track carriages. It had a 56-calibre air-cooled barrel firing a 2.62lb (1.19kg) high-explosive projectile to a maximum vertical range of 6,200yd (5,670m), although practical fire missions involved were limited to a maximum of just under 4,000yd (3,657m).

Ammunition was fed into the gun in four-round clips to be fired at a cyclic rate of 120 rounds-per-minute. Muzzle velocity was 2,600ft/sec (792m/sec).

40mm Gun Motor Carriage T54

The 40mm Gun Motor Carriage T54 was based on a much-modified Half-Track Personnel Carrier M3. The 40mm M1 gun was placed on the flat open rear of the vehicle to provide a full arc (360°) of fire, barrel elevation being from 0° to +85°. There was no protection for the crew and ammunition stowage was minimal. Both limitations were considered as unimportant as far as the T54 was concerned as it was meant purely as a platform for firing trials.

The firing trials demonstrated that the combination of M1 gun and M3 half-track was unsatisfactory. The chassis was overloaded and became unstable when firing, both factors that continued to plague the 40mm GMC programme.

A possible short-term solution to the stability problems was the introduction of the 40mm Gun Motor Carriage T54E1. The vehicle was fitted with stabilising outriggers and jacks combined with a device that isolated the vehicle's suspension springing prior to firing the gun. Although designed for rapid deployment the outriggers took too long to position and did not work very well either. The instability problem remained.

The T54 and T54E1 models were abandoned, only one example of each being constructed and tested.

40mm Gun Motor Carriage T59

Engineering data provided by the T54 project was introduced into the next development stage, the 40mm Gun Motor Carriage T59. It was hoped that revised outriggers and a new suspension isolator system would overcome the problems of the T54/T54E1 but in the event the T59 proved to be just as unstable as the previous model. An attempt to introduce a revised fire-control system on the 40mm Gun Motor Carriage T59E1 fared no better so the T59 project was abruptly cancelled.

It was intended that the T59's outriggers would be used with an associated vehicle, the

Above:
In an attempt to cure firing stability problems outriggers and a revised suspension were fitted to this T59. But it was no better than the earlier T54 model and did not progress beyond prototype stage. *(TG)*

Far left:
Overhead view of the 40mm Gun Motor Carriage T54 showing how the bulk of the 40mm M1 Gun occupied much of the available space. *(TM)*

Above: Perhaps the most outlandish of all the half-track weapon carrier series was the 40mm Gun Motor Carriage T68 but it remained at the experimental model stage as the twin 40mm M1 Guns severely overloaded the chassis. *(TG)*

Half-Track Instrument Carrier T18. This carried a British-designed electro-mechanical prediction system known as the Kerrison Predictor. The T18 was to carry this device, known in the US Army as the Director M5, also a Generator Unit M5 to power the director and the associated electrical cables. These connected the T18 to the T59, the two vehicles working in conjunction. The T18 went the same way as the T59 carriage and was abandoned.

40mm Multiple Gun Motor Carriage T60

Although this project almost reciprocates the Multiple Gun Motor Carriage (MGMC) half-track series, of which more later, it is included here to continue the 40mm GMC narrative. It concerned the 40mm Multiple Gun Motor Carriage T60.

The T60 project was a close associate of the T59 but with the addition of two .50-calibre M2 HB machine guns. The intention was that the two machine guns and the 40mm gun would be co-axial, the machine guns firing tracer ammunition until they came to bear on the target. Only then would the 40mm gun be fired. The T60 had many problems, not least because the firing ballistics of the machine guns and the main gun did not match. In addition, the recoil instability problems remained. By the time the T60 programme was about to commence the mobile 40mm air defence requirement had been met by entry into service of the Twin 40mm Gun Motor Carriage M19 based on the chassis of the Light Tank M24 (Chaffee).

The T60 project therefore lapsed, but not before work had commenced on the 40mm Multiple Gun Motor Carriage T65E1. This was a development of the T60 with a revised shield assembly and revised ammunition stowage. It was cancelled along with the T60 programme.

40mm Gun Motor Carriage T68

The inherent problems of the 40mm Gun Motor Carriage series did not prevent the appearance of what was probably the most outlandish gun and half-track combination of them all, the 40mm Gun Motor Carriage T68.

The T68 featured a gun mounting proposal from the American Ordnance Company. It proposed that two 40mm M1 guns would be mounted one over the other in a special mounting, their elevating axis well to the rear of each gun. This odd arrangement dictated the use of an equilibrator housing located over the guns to balance their combined weight.

The M3 chassis used for the T68 was completely open-topped to the extent that even the driver's cab protection was removed. A pilot model was constructed and submitted to the US Army's Anti-aircraft Artillery Board during June 1943. It did not like what it saw and the T68 project was cancelled. No doubt it did not like the bulk and open nature of the vehicle, while the usual firing stability problems would no doubt have been amplified.

40mm Gun Motor Carriage T1

The 40mm Gun Motor Carriage T1 project is not really part of the US half-track narrative but is mentioned here purely to complete the 40mm M1 gun motor carriage story. It concerned a May 1941 proposal to place a 40mm M1 gun, plus its associated fire director and power generator, on a single half-track chassis.

The chassis concerned could have been termed as a three-quarters track chassis as the track length was much greater than for the M2/M3 series. Designated the Half-Track Chassis T3, it was devised by the Mack Manufacturing Company of Allentown, Pennsylvania. The top of the T3 chassis was completely open, including the driver's position, while the engine was at the rear. A Director M5 was positioned next to the driver, the gun was mounted in the centre of the vehicle and the generator overhung the rear. Despite extensive testing the Mack chassis was the source of constant mechanical troubles. It also proved difficult to integrate the gun and director into a fully functioning system. In the end the mechanical problems relating

Below: Although not really a part of the half-track weapon carrier series, the short-lived 40mm Gun Motor Carriage T1 was an unsuccessful attempt to make the 40mm M1 Gun more mobile. *(TG)*

Above:
The Multiple Gun Motor Carriage T10 was intended to carry two 20mm cannon of a type to be decided. These were to be carried on a Maxson M33 air-defence turret mounting on an M3 chassis but the project was cancelled. *(TM)*

to the chassis proved too severe to rectify economically so the project was terminated without fully evaluating the performance of the gun.

Multiple Gun Motor Carriages

The Multiple Gun Motor Carriage concept embraced several types of combat vehicle other than half-tracks but all had an underlying origin. US Army observers in France during 1940 had noted the severe damage inflicted by low-flying German aircraft on French field formations, their reports resulting in a search for some form of mobile, low-level air-defence programme to defend their armed forces in the field. For the US armed forces of 1940 there was only one low-level air-defence weapon available, the .50-calibre M2 machine gun in either air- or water-cooled form. It was appreciated that the chances of such weapons inflicting significant damage to fast, low-flying aircraft were very limited but it was reasoned that if multiple gun barrels were used those chances were much improved as, theoretically, more bullets would be available to strike the target. The Multiple Gun Motor Carriage was born and half-tracks were the chosen vehicle.

The machine gun involved in virtually all these multiple gun carriages was the Browning .50-calibre M2 machine gun in one form or another. Experience with the air-cooled M2 HB proved that it was every bit as effective as the water-cooled model, intended to fire long bursts, and was lighter and easier to maintain. Most of the guns fitted on the multiple gun carriages were actually the M2 HB TT (TT denoting Tank Turret as they had a remote control, solenoid-operated trigger). In this form each gun weighed 81lb (36.74kg). Other than that they were exactly the same gun as on the flexible mountings mentioned in the Armament section.

When the Multiple Gun Motor Carriage concept was first adopted it had to be determined what the optimum multiple gun configuration should be, beginning with two guns on a single mounting.

Above:
The Multiple Gun Motor Carriage M14 was the same as the M13 type but built on the IHC M5 chassis instead of the M3. It carried two .50in M2 machine guns. *(TM)*

Left:
Overhead view of the Multiple Gun Motor Carriage M13 built on an M3 chassis. *(TM)*

Above:
While the Multiple Gun Motor Carriage M14 was quite successful in its air-defence role, most were passed to the British Army who promptly removed the guns and found other uses for the M5 chassis. *(TM)*

Multiple Gun Motor Carriage T1 series

The prime purpose of the vehicles in the Multiple Gun Motor Carriage T1 series was to determine exactly what form an air-defence gun and vehicle combination would take. Three main trials vehicles were involved.

The Multiple Gun Motor Carriage T1E1 was an M2 half-track provided with an open Bendix power-operated turret, mounting two guns.

The Multiple Gun Motor Carriage T1E2 again involved an M2 half-track, this time with a twin-gun mounting from the Maxson Company.

The Multiple Gun Motor Carriage T1E3 was another machine gun combination, this time with an aircraft-type, power-operated turret designed by the Ordnance Department at Wright Field, Ohio.

Of these three the T1E2 with the Maxson Mounting proved to be the most efficient for the gunner to aim at the sudden appearance of a target so it was standardised, after some slight modifications, as the Twin Cal .50 Machine Gun Mount M33. To provide as much space as possible the M33 was mounted on a Half-Track Personnel Carrier M3 which then became the Multiple Gun Motor Carriage T1E4. It was standardised as the Multiple Gun Motor Carriage M13 in July, 1942.

Multiple Gun Motor Carriage M13

The so-called Maxson Mounting M33 was electrically powered, with the gunner seated between the two machine guns and behind a .25in (6.35mm) thick armour plate shield. The guns were power traversed on a turntable at a rate of from 0 to 72° per second and elevated from -11.5° to +90°. The sides and rear of the vehicle had to be hinged downwards to allow the maximum gun depression. Minimum elevation was limited to +10° over the frontal arc.

The Multiple Gun Motor Carriage M13 carried a crew of five. There was no provision for any secondary armament as the two machine guns were just as effective against land targets as they were against aircraft. A total of 5,000 rounds of .50-calibre ammunition were

Above:
The Multiple Gun Motor Carriage M16 carried four .50in M2 machine guns in place of the original two with only slight modifications to the Maxson mount. *(TM)*

carried. A power generator was also fitted to recharge the batteries of the M33 mounting.

Production of the M13 was carried out by White. A total of 1,103 was manufactured during 1943. Of these, ten were diverted to the Lend-Lease Program, all for the British Army.

Multiple Gun Motor Carriage M14

Such was the demand for the Multiple Gun Motor Carriage M13 that International Harvester (IHC) became involved, the M33 Maxson Mounting being mounted on a Half-Track Car M5 chassis. Apart from the IHC-related vehicle differences, as outlined under the Description chapter, the M14 was exactly the same as the M13.

The production total for IHC was 1,605, five being built during late 1942 and the rest completed during 1943. Of these only five were retained for US Army use, the other 1,600 being passed under the Lend-Lease Program to the British. By the time they reached British hands it was considered that the need for low-level air defence vehicles was no longer desperate. As a result the British removed the machine gun mountings from many of their M14s and converted them to other roles, usually as personnel carriers or command vehicles.

Multiple Gun Motor Carriage M16

To continue the half-track and machine gun mobile mounting story the next phase came about as a result of some clever engineering by the Maxson Company whereby the twin-gun M33 gun mounting was redesigned to carry four .50-calibre M2 HB TT machine guns. The result became the Multiple Cal .50 Machine Gun Mount M45 and was tested on an M2 half-track as the Multiple Gun Motor Carriage T58. Following tests it was decided that the Half-Track Personnel Carrier M3 would provide a better platform for the mounting and this combination became the Multiple Gun Motor Carriage M16.

The Ordnance Department had already been developing its own four-gun mounting

Multiple Gun Motor Carriage M16

© 2004 Mike Rose.

Right:
A close-up of the front of a quadruple Maxson Mount with the distinctive ammunition boxes. The vehicle is a Multiple Gun Motor Carriage M16. *(JBn)*

Above:
The crew of a Multiple Gun Motor Carriage M16 ready to engage any aircraft that might appear – note the name ('Hilter's Hearse') painted on the side of the vehicle. *(TM)*

Left:
Rear view of a Multiple Gun Motor Carriage M16 Maxson Mount showing the auxiliary generator carried to recharge the batteries used to power the

Right:
One of the trials models that led to the Multiple Gun Motor Carriage M16 was the Multiple Gun Motor Carriage T37E1, with four .50in M2 machine guns arranged in line and behind a circular gun shield. This model did not enter production. *(TG)*

on the Multiple Gun Motor Carriage T37 and T37E1. On the M3-based T37 the .50-calibre machine guns were arranged in a 'square' configuration, while on the T37E1 they were all side-by-side. The arrival of the M55 Maxson Mounting caused the T37/T37E1 project to be abandoned.

To return to the M16, its development meant that the earlier M13 and M14 carriages were immediately reclassified as Substitute Standard, all production switching to the M16. Each M2 HB TT gun could fire at a cyclic rate of 400 to 500 rounds-per-minute; when firing all four guns together the rate was up to 2,000rpm, a rate capable of inflicting serious - if not fatal - damage to any low-flying aircraft. The only degrading change from the earlier M33 mounting was that, due to the extra weights involved, the traverse rate was reduced to 60° per second. The ammunition load for each M16 remained at 5,000 rounds and the crew strength remained at five. A fully-loaded M16 weighed approximately 8.84 tons (8,981kg).

Total production of the Multiple Gun Motor Carriage M16 was 2,877, with 2,323 built during 1943 and 554 during 1944. Only 72 of these went to the Lend-Lease Program, two of them to the British Army which by 1943 no longer felt it had any pressing need for low-level air defence vehicles. The remaining 70 went to the Free French Army.

After 1945 refurbished M16s destined to be distributed as US military aid were redesignated as Multiple Gun Motor Carriage M16A1 or M16A2. These were not used by the US armed forces.

Multiple Gun Motor Carriage M17

The .50 Multiple Gun Motor Carriage development history came to an end with the Multiple Gun Motor Carriage M17. This was virtually the same vehicle as the M16 but based on the IHC Half-Track Car M5. Production of these vehicles reached 1,000 and they were the last half-tracks manufactured by IHC. The first 400 were completed during 1943 and the

Above:
The Multiple Gun Motor Carriage T28, shown here without the two .50in M2 water-cooled machine guns installed on either side of the 37mm M1A2 gun. This model was based on the M2 half-track chassis. *(TM)*

remaining 600 during 1944. The entire M17 output went to the Soviet Union through the Lend-Lease Program.

Multiple Gun Motor Carriage M15

The Multiple Gun Motor Carriage M15 was a combination of a 37mm Automatic Gun M1A2 and two .50-calibre M2 machine guns on a common co-axial mounting, all carried on a single mounting, the Combination Gun Mount M54. Development began with the Multiple Gun Motor Carriage T28 based on an M2 half-track chassis, the machine guns being water-cooled. The weight and space demands of the load indicated that an M3 half-track chassis should be used instead and this was introduced with the Multiple Gun Motor Carriage T28E1, all of the vehicle's side and rear armour being removed and the gun placed behind a prominent shield. Following slight modifications to the shield and some other details the T28E1 was standardised as the Multiple Gun Motor Carriage M15.

The 37mm gun carried by the M15 was yet another Browning product dating from 1925. Browning died soon after a prototype had been completed and the 37mm programme lapsed until 1940 when final improvements were introduced and it was standardised as the 37mm Automatic Gun M1A2 and Carriage M3A1. The top section of the Carriage M3A1 was used as the basis for the Combination Gun Mount M54. The Gun M1A2 fired a 1.34lb (608g) high-explosive projectile at a muzzle velocity of 2,800ft/sec (853m/sec) to a maximum vertical range of 3,860yd (3,530m). The cyclic rate of fire was 120rpm. Armour-piercing ammunition could also be fired.

On paper the performance of the 37mm Gun M1A2 was very similar to that of the Bofors Gun but in practice the 37mm ammunition proved under-powered. But the US Army selected the 37mm gun before it tested the 40mm Bofors and ordered the 37mm M1A2 into large-scale production. With large numbers coming off established production lines it took a considerable effort to convert to

(cont page 91)

SHELL, FIXED, HE-T, SD, M54, with fuze, PD, M56, for 37mm Gun

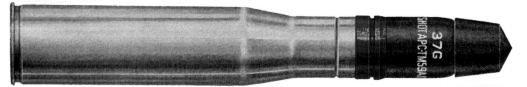

SHELL, FIXED, APC-T, M59A1, steel case, for 37mm Gun

SHELL, FIXED, TP-T, M55A1, with fuze, dummy, M50, for 37mm Gun

SHELL, HE, M56, with fuze, TSQ, M77, for 81mm mortar

SHELL, SMOKE, WP, M57, with fuze, PD, M53A1, for 81mm mortar

SHELL, ILLUMINATING, M301, with fuze, time, M84, for 81mm mortar

SHELL, HE, M43A1, with fuze, PD, M52A1, for 81mm mortar

© 2004 Nigel Pell.

Left:
A pilot model of the Multiple Gun Motor Carriage M15 fitted with the 37mm gun and two air-cooled .50in machine guns protected by a T28E1 pattern gun shield. *(TM)*

Below:
A Multiple Gun Motor Carriage M15A1 with the loader holding one of the ten-round 37mm ammunition clips. *(TM)*

Left:
Multiple Gun Motor Carriage M15, identifiable by the twin-machine guns being located above the main 37mm gun. *(TM)*

Far left:
A Multiple Gun Motor Carriage M15A1 somewhere in Northern France, late 1944. Note the trailer used to carry extra ammunition and the crews' kit. *(TM)*

Below:
The T60 MGMC with 40mm Bofors and twin .50 calibre M2HB machine guns. The stabilising out-riggers are extended. *(TM)*

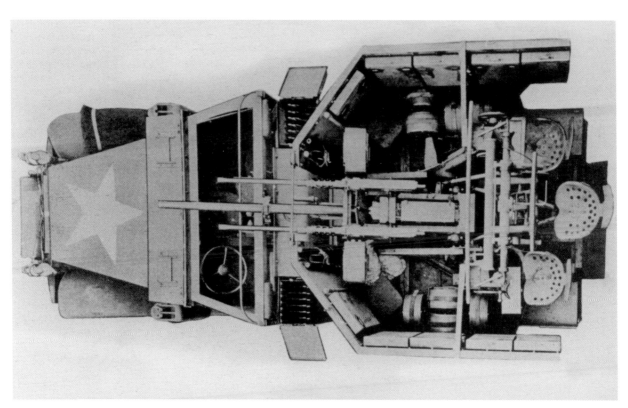

Left:
The Multiple Gun Motor Carriage T1E1 was one of the 1941 pilot models that led to the M16 series. It had two .50in machine guns in a Bendix aircraft-type powered turret. This was carried on an M2 chassis. *(TG)*

Far left:
A Multiple Gun Motor Carriage M15 from above showing the ammunition stowage location close behind the driving cab area. *(TM)*

the 40mm gun and air defence guns were sorely needed in the front lines. In the end, both were used in service until 1945.

On the manually powered Combination Gun Mount M54 the intention was that a target would be engaged by one of the machine guns until the tracers were seen to be striking the target. The main 37mm gun and the second machine gun would then be fired together at the target. In practice gunners usually fired all three guns at the same time. The Multiple Gun Motor Carriage M15 proved to be a highly effective combination and was deployed on many battlefronts.

The M15 was replaced in production by the Multiple Gun Motor Carriage M15A1 which differed by having a Combination Mount M54 with a revised fire control system. The M15A1 was slightly lighter than the M15 and was considered to be a more stable vehicle. It was also easier to conceal, thanks mainly to the lower height of the gun. More user-friendly measures were added to assist the crew of seven in their tasks. On the M15 the two .50-calibre machine guns were above the 37mm gun. On the M15A1 they were below the gun.

A total of 680 examples of the M15 were manufactured, 80 during 1942 and the other

Left:
A late-production Multiple Gun Motor Carriage M15A1 showing the location of the two machine guns beneath the line of the main 37mm M1A1 gun armament. *(TM)*

600 during 1943. For the M15A1 the final production total was 1,652, with 1,052 being built during 1943 and the final 600 during 1944. The only Lend-Lease Program record was for 100, almost certainly M15s, all of them being sent to the Soviet Union. Many more were distributed as US military aid after 1945.

Multiple Gun Motor Carriage T10 and T10E1

With the multiple machine gun carriages the limitations of the .50 machine gun ammunition were that it lacked a high-explosive payload and the effective range was too short. To overcome these shortcomings recourse was made during July 1941 to replacing the machine guns by 20mm cannon. Two cannon could be fitted on a Maxson machine gun mounting. The exact model of cannon was never finally established, types being investigated including Hispano-Suiza, Oerlikon and the 20mm Automatic Gun AN-M1 or AN-M2. All types of these cannon were tested on a modified M3 half-track chassis (20mm Multiple Gun Motor Carriage T10) or a modified M16 (20mm Multiple Gun Motor Carriage T10E1).

In the event the development programme, although completed, did not result in any production contracts, although many of the features of the 20mm mountings were introduced after 1945.

Half-Track Trucks

To complete the US half-track story mention must be made of the intended replacements. They were the Half-Track Truck T16, T17 and T19. These were totally new and heavier designs with increased track lengths and were mainly intended to be artillery tractors. Most of their development was carried out during 1942 and 1943 by Autocar and White (the T16 and T17) and the Mack Manufacturing Company (the T19). The decision to replace half-tracks with fully-tracked carriers and tractors for future requirements meant that all three projects were terminated.

Far left:
The Multiple Gun Motor Carriage T10 did not enter production as preference was given to heavy machine guns for air defence over the slower-firing 20mm cannon. *(TM)*

Left:
An experimental M3 half-track fitted with a mine flail installation. The flails were driven from the main engine. The vehicle was not used operationally. *(TG)*

Right:
Although not intended to be a weapons carrier, the Half-Track Car T16 was an early 1942 trials vehicle based on an M2 chassis with an armoured roof. It did not enter production. *(TG)*

Right:
Rear view of the Half-Track Car T16 showing the armoured roof and the open upper sides. *(TM)*

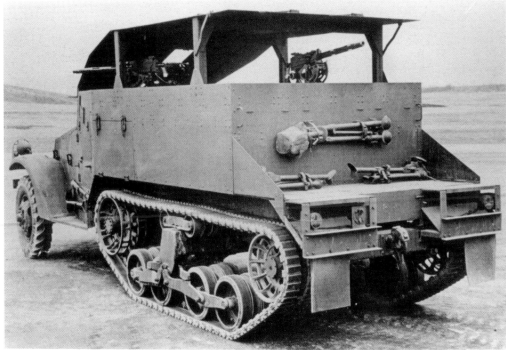

Left:
The Half-Track Truck T16 was one of at least three models intended to ultimately replace the existing half-track series. Built by the Diamond T Motor Company the project was terminated after only two examples had been built. *(TM)*

Above: With the end of the war in sight, M3A1s enter the Ruhr region of Germany during March 1945. *(TM)*